"WALKER CONTINUES TO ENCHANT."
—*San Jose Mercury News*

"Illuminating . . . Alice Walker emerges from these pages as a knowing 'almost elder'—thoughtful, funny, gentle, yet a fighter for those causes in which she believes."

—*Atlanta Journal & Constitution*

"Walker writes full-heartedly about her life as an activist and her faith in the human heart, unabashedly revealing her thoughts on issues both private and public."

—*Chicago Tribune*

"Impassioned . . . Walker tackles more than a dozen hot-button issues. . . . One can't help feeling charged up, sharing the range of Walker's energy and involvement, her refusal to do anything half-heartedly."

—*St. Louis Post-Dispatch*

"Create[s] the feel of a conversation over a cup of tea . . . Her family stories interwoven with her activism and experiences read seamlessly together; one logically forming and feeding the other."

—*The Seattle Times*

"Heartfelt and compassionate."

—*San Francisco Examiner & Chronicle*

Please turn the page for more reviews . . .

"REVEALING . . .

Ms. Walker again ushers the reader into her internal world and makes us privy to her objectives, thoughts, and feelings. . . . [She] reveals herself as a multidimensional, compassionate warrior, fighting with her pen, heart, and sometimes her body in the cause of black and other oppressed peoples, the poor, women, and the planet she loves. . . . The activism on display throughout the book has a tempered yet incisive quality that characterizes the best of Ms. Walker's fiction and poetry."

—*The Dallas Morning News*

"More than just a collection of engaging thoughts and daring philosophies, *Anything We Love Can Be Saved* is a portrait of courage, joy, sorrow, heavy letdowns, and much applauded celebrations."

—*African Sun Times*

"Walker provides an inspiring look at her life in action. This powerful new collection contains essays, poems, letters, and speeches, some public pronouncements, many personal reflections, all illuminating the heart and soul of a writer-activist in this age of widespread ennui and apathy."

—*The Seattle Post-Intelligencer*

"Frankly emotional . . . Heartfelt . . . At the center of each narrative is Walker's belief that every attempt to change the world for the better, no matter how modest, is transcendent."

—*Booklist*

"Walker's commitment to activism shines forth convincingly in this wide-ranging collection. . . . Constantly testing and stretching her readers' imaginations and boundaries, Walker expresses her warmth, her anger, her optimism in this provocative, lively collection."

—*Publishers Weekly*

Anything We Love Can Be Saved

Anything We Love Can Be Saved

A WRITER'S ACTIVISM

Alice Walker

BALLANTINE BOOKS
THE BALLANTINE PUBLISHING GROUP
NEW YORK

In memory of Ken Saro-Wiwa and
in solidarity with the peoples
of Cuba and Tibet
and
for Mumia
and
Mu

THE PLACE IN THE WAYS

Having come to this place
I set out once again
on the dark and marvelous way
from where I began:
belief in the love of the world,
woman, spirit, and man.

Having failed in all things
I enter a new age
seeing the old ways as toys,
the houses of a stage
painted and long forgot;
and I find love and rage.

Rage for the world as it is
but for what it may be
more love now than last year
and always less self-pity
since I know in a clearer light
the strength of the mystery.

And at this place in the ways
I wait for song.
My poem-hand still, on the paper,
all night long.
Poems in throat and hand, asleep,
and my storm beating strong!

—MURIEL RUKEYSER

MY
ANTHEM

Joie de vivre, joie de vivre
Joie de vivre, over me

And before I'll be a slave
I'll be dancing on my grave
And go home

to my soul
and be free

—*To the tune of "Oh, Freedom"*

May Poole.
A precious heritage.

Acknowledgments

The first person I must thank for my belief in activism is my great-great-great-great-grandmother May Poole. She lived, enslaved in the North American South, throughout the nineteenth century, dying at the age of a hundred and twenty-five when my father was a boy of eleven. So strong was her spirit, and so clearly did I reflect some of it, that the elderly white woman to whom she'd been given as a wedding gift over three-quarters of a century before recognized me as her descendant from an article and photograph in the local newspaper. When I went to visit this aged woman and her husband in a nursing home before their deaths, she gave me the only photograph of May Poole in existence. In it she is undeniably old, in her nineties, according to the elderly couple, and leaning on a stick. But in her look I can still see the attitude and courage that made it possible for her to attend the funerals of almost everyone who'd ever owned her.

I thank my mother for mothering all the children within her reach who needed it, and especially for attempting to instill spiritual values, which she did by holding Bible studies with the neighborhood children in her living room. I could see, because she believed it, that every child is precious and each one must be sheltered, instructed in whatever broadens his or her appreciation of life, and physically fed, without question. Nor did she discriminate on the basis of size, color, shape of head, or degree of intelligence. She never heard of Marx, not even from me. Yet she lived the axiom "From each according to his (her) abilities, to each according to his (her) needs." And proved that Christ was right when he said, "Suffer little children to come unto me, for of such is the kingdom of heaven." For her activity on behalf of children and the community resulted in making my mother a very happy, light-filled woman. She spent many years in heaven, long before she died. This was, daily, simply amazing to see.

I thank my father for his wonderful sense of humor, which effortlessly undermined the racist nonsense that passed for white supremacist wisdom while I was growing up. He would have shared a laugh with Zora Neale Hurston, who said, when stopped for going through a red light in the segregated South, "Well, I saw all the white people going on the green, so I thought the red must be for me." He too had a story for every occasion and taught me it is possible for the word to become sharper than the sword.

I thank Trellie Jeffers and Mrs. Brown and Mr. Roberson of my high school, as well as our thoughtful, quietly heroic principal, Mr. McGlockton, for holding high expectations for me, and for diligently preparing me to encounter the world beyond my small community. Their simple belief in doing their jobs properly, and with concern for my welfare after I left their instruction, was activism at its very best.

I thank Howard Zinn and Staughton Lynd, radical activists, historians, and loving souls, for their example of how to agitate where you are; at Spelman College, where they were my teachers, among other places. Along with Malcolm X, Martin Luther King, Jr., Fannie Lou Hamer, and Rosa Parks, they represent activism at its most contagious, because it is always linked to celebration and joy. I also thank Che Guevara and Fidel Castro for their daring as revolutionaries, but also for their writing and their speeches. Empowerment of the poor—through education, health care, and adequate housing—is always foremost in their thought; I have found this reassuring over the years as the poor and weak have steadily increased in numbers around the world, and the wealthy and politically powerful have designed ever more clever ways to humiliate and exploit them.

I thank my editor, Kate Medina, for her understanding. I thank Virginia Avery, copy editor, for her thoughtful precision. I thank my agent, Wendy Weil, for helping me find a net.

I thank my friend and administrative assistant, Joan Miura, for her unfailing courtesy, kindness, and love.

I am especially fortunate to have the example of activist teachers and friends. Efua Dorkenoo, Pratibha Parmar, Mel Leventhal, Angela Davis, John Trudell, Tillie Olsen, Marian Wright Edelman, June Jordan, Bernice Johnson Reagon, Clarissa Pinkola Estés, Jean Shinoda Bolen, Wilma Mankiller, Gloria Steinem, Dennis Banks, Archie Roach, Estér Hernandez, Tracy Chapman, Samuel Zan, Pema Chödrön, and Nawal El Saadawi, among others, are deeply thanked, and profoundly cherished "for being there."

Contents

Illustrations

Alice Walker following her arrest at the Concord Naval Weapons Station in June 1987 during a demonstration protesting the base's alleged role in the shipment of arms to Central America.

JON MCNALLY

Introduction:
Belief in the Love of the World

This book begins with the essay "The Only Reason You Want to Go to Heaven Is That You Have Been Driven Out of Your Mind (Off Your Land and Out of Your Lover's Arms): Clear Seeing Inherited Religion and Reclaiming the Pagan Self." In it I explore my awareness, beginning in childhood, of the limitations of the patriarchal Christianity into which I was born; as well as my realization, over time, that my most cherished instinctual, natural self, the pagan self, was in danger of dying from its oppression by an ideology that had been forced on my ancestors, under threat of punishment or death, and was, for the most part, alien to me. That essay, which was delivered in a seminary in April of 1995, is followed by one about a meeting with people working toward the abolition of female genital mutilation in Bolgatanga, Northern Ghana, that occurred in April of 1996. The book ends with an essay entitled "My Mother's Blue Bowl," which grew out of my grieving for my mother after her death, in 1993, and the eventual solace I have taken in memories of all the ways in which she sacrificed to give me life, and *fullness* of life.

Preceding that essay, there is a letter to President Clinton protesting the recent tightening of the thirty-seven-year-old U.S. blockade of Cuba, which threatens everyone in that island country with starvation. There are pieces on the resurrection of Zora Neale Hurston, the trials of Winnie Mandela, the experience of being both praised and banned as a writer, and the joy of discovering the Goddess in places we've been ashamed to look. There is also an essay on the sustaining miracle of Sweet Honey in the Rock, another on the beauty of dreadlocks, and another on how the life of an activist can be hard on her cat. I also write about our timid acceptance, as women, of language that "disappears" us, of the strengthening that comes from renewing family connections, and of the bittersweet struggle involved in mothering a child.

My activism—cultural, political, spiritual—is rooted in my love of nature and my delight in human beings. It is when people are at peace, content, *full,* that they are most likely to meet my expectation, selfish, no doubt, that they be a generous, joyous, even entertaining experience for me. I believe people exist to be enjoyed, much as a restful or engaging view might be. As the ocean or drifting clouds might be. Or as if they were the human equivalent of melons, mangoes, or any other kind of attractive, seductive fruit. When I am in the presence of other human beings I want to revel in their creative and intellectual fullness, their uninhibited social warmth. I want their precious human radiance to wrap me in light. I do not want fear of war or starvation or bodily mutilation to steal both my pleasure in them and their own birthright. Everything I would like other people to be for me, I want to be for them.

I have been an activist all my adult life, though I have sometimes felt embarrassed to call myself one. In the Sixties, many of us were plagued by the notion that, given the magnitude of the task before us—the dismantling of American apartheid—our individual acts were puny. There was also the apparent reality that the most committed, most directly confrontational people suffered more. The most "revolutionary" often ended up severely beaten, in prison, or dead. Shot down in front of their children, blown up in cars or in church, run over by racist drunks, raped and thrown in the river.

In Mississippi, where I lived from 1967 to 1974, people who challenged the system anticipated menace, battery, even murder, every day. In this context, I sometimes felt ashamed that my contributions at the time were not more radical. I taught in two local black colleges, I wrote about the Movement, and I created tiny history booklets which were used to teach the teachers of children enrolled in Head Start. And, of course, I was interracially married, which was illegal. It was perhaps in Mississippi during those years that I understood how the daily news of disaster can become, for the spirit, a numbing assault, and that one's own activism, however modest, fighting against this tide of death, provides at least the possibility of generating a different kind of "news." A "news" that empowers rather than defeats.

There is always a moment in any kind of struggle when one feels in full bloom. Vivid. Alive. One might be blown to bits in such a moment and still be at peace. Martin Luther King, Jr., at the mountaintop. Gandhi dying with the name of God on his lips. Sojourner Truth baring her breasts at a women's rights convention in 1851. Harriet Tubman exposing her revolver to some of the slaves she had freed, who, fearing an unknown freedom, looked longingly backward to their captivity, thereby endangering the freedom of all. To be such a person or to witness anyone at this moment of transcendent presence is to know that what is human is linked, by a daring compassion, to what is divine. During my years of being close to people engaged in changing the world I have seen fear turn into courage. Sorrow into joy. Funerals into celebrations. Because whatever the consequences, people, standing side by side, have expressed who they really are, and that ultimately they believe in the love of the world and each other enough *to be that*—which is the foundation of activism.

It has become a common feeling, I believe, as we have watched our heroes falling over the years, that our own small stone of activism, which might not seem to measure up to the rugged boulders of heroism we have so admired, is a paltry offering toward the building of an edifice of hope. Many who believe this choose to withhold their offerings out of shame.

This is the tragedy of our world.

For we can do nothing substantial toward changing our course on the planet, a destructive one, without rousing ourselves, individual by individual, and bringing our small, imperfect stones to the pile.

In this regard, I have a story to tell.

In the mid-Sixties during a voter-registration campaign in south Georgia, my canvassing partner, Beverly, a local black teenager, was arrested on a bogus moving-violation charge. This was meant to intimidate her, "show her her place," and terrify her family. Those of us who feared for her safety during the night held a vigil outside the jail. I remember the raw vulnerability I felt as the swaggering state troopers—each of them three times Beverly's size, and mine—stomped in and out of the building, scowling at us. The feeling of solidarity with Beverly and our friends was strong, but also the feeling of being alone, as it occurred to me that not even my parents knew where I was. We were black and very young: we knew no one in White America paid the slightest attention to the deaths of such as us. It was partly because of this that we sometimes resented the presence of the white people who came to stand, and take their chances, with us. I was one of those to whom such resentment came easily.

I especially resented blond Paul from Minnesota, whose Aryan appearance meant, when he was not with us, freedom and almost worship in the race-obsessed South. I had treated him with coolness since the day we met. We certainly did not invite him to our vigil. And yet, at just the moment I felt most downhearted, I heard someone coming along the street in our direction, whistling. A moment later Paul appeared. Still whistling a Movement spiritual that sounded strange, even comical, on his lips, he calmly took his place beside us. Knowing his Nordic presence meant a measure of safety for us, and without being asked, he offered it. This remains a moment as bright as any I recall from that time.

As a poet and writer, I used to think being an activist and writing about it "demoted" me to the level of "mere journalist." Now I know that, as with the best journalists, activism is often my muse. And that it is organic. Grounded in my mother's love of beauty, the well-tended garden and the carefully swept yard, her satisfaction in knowing everyone in her environment was sheltered and fed; and in my father's insistence, even as a poor black man, easily "disappeared" for any political activity, that black people deserved the vote, black children deserved decent schools.

All we own, at least for the short time we have it, is our life. With it we write what we come to know of the world. I believe the Earth is good. That people, untortured by circumstance or fate, are also good. I do not believe the people of the world are naturally my enemies, or that animals, including snakes, are, or that Nature is. Whenever I experience evil, and it is not, unfortunately, uncommon to experience it in these times, my deepest feeling is disappointment. I have learned to accept the fact that we risk disappointment, disillusionment, even despair, every time we act. Every time we decide to believe the world can be better. Every time we decide to trust others to be as noble as we think they are. And that there might be *years* during which our grief is equal to, or even greater than, our hope. The alternative, however, not to act, and therefore to miss experiencing other people at their best, reaching toward their fullness, has never appealed to me.

I have learned other things: One is the futility of expecting anyone, including oneself, to be perfect. People who go about seeking to change the world, to diminish suffering, to demonstrate any kind of enlightenment, are often as flawed as anybody else. Sometimes more so. But it is the awareness of having faults, I think, and the knowledge that this links us to everyone on earth, that opens us to courage and compassion. It occurs to me often that many of those I deeply love *are* flawed. They might actually have said or done some of the mean things I've *felt,* heard, read about, or feared. But it is their struggle with the flaw, surprisingly endearing, *and the going on anyhow,* that is part of what I cherish in them.

Sometimes our stones are, to us, misshapen, odd. Their color seems off. Their singing, like Paul's whistling, comical and strange. Presenting them, we perceive our own imperfect nakedness. But also, paradoxically, the wholeness, the rightness, of it. In the collective vulnerability of presence, we learn not to be afraid.

In this book I am writing about the bright moments one can experience at the pile. Of how even the smallest stone glistens with tears, yes, but also from the light of being seen, and loved for simply being there.

PART ONE

The Only Reason You Want to Go to Heaven . . .

The church of my childhood, where I first, before birth, encountered my beloved community. (I heard singing!) The simplicity and sweetness of this structure, and the warmth of the human relationships fashioned within its walls and yard, have influenced every aspect of my life.

PHOTO BY ALICE WALKER, 1972

The Only Reason You Want to Go to Heaven Is That You Have Been Driven Out of Your Mind

(Off Your Land and Out of Your Lover's Arms)

CLEAR SEEING INHERITED RELIGION AND RECLAIMING THE PAGAN SELF

Unto the woman God said: I will greatly multiply thy sorrow and thy conception; in sorrow thou shalt bring forth children; and thy desire shall be to thy husband, and he shall rule over thee.
—GENESIS

In my novel *The Color Purple* Celie and Shug discuss, as all thoughtful humans must, the meaning of God. Shug says, "I believe God is everything that is, ever was or ever will be." Celie, raised to worship a God that resembles "the little fat white man who works in the bank," only bigger and bearded, learns to agree. I agree also. It was years after writing these words for Shug that I discovered they were also spoken, millennia ago, by Isis, ancient

Goddess of Africa, who, as an African, can be said to be a spiritual mother of us all.

There is a special grief felt by the children and grandchildren of those who were forbidden to read, forbidden to explore, forbidden to question or to know. Looking back on my parents' and grandparents' lives, I have often felt overwhelmed, helpless, as I've examined history and society, and especially religion, with them in mind, and have seen how they were manipulated away from a belief in their own judgment and faith in themselves.

It is painful to realize they were forever trying to correct a "flaw"—that of being black, female, human—that did not exist, except as "men of God," but really men of greed, misogyny, and violence, defined it. What a burden to think one is conceived in sin rather than in pleasure; that one is born into evil rather than into joy. In my work, I speak to my parents and to my most distant ancestors about what I myself have found as an Earthling growing naturally out of the Universe. I create characters who sometimes speak in the language of immediate ancestors, characters who are not passive but active in the discovery of what is vital and real in this world. Characters who explore what it would feel like not to be imprisoned by the hatred of women, the love of violence, and the destructiveness of greed taught to human beings as the "religion" by which they must guide their lives.

What is happening in the world more and more is that people are attempting to decolonize their spirits. A crucial act of empowerment, one that might return reverence to the Earth, thereby saving it, in this fearful-of-Nature, spiritually colonized age.

An example of this decolonization occurs in *The Color Purple*: Shug, the pagan, discusses the nature of God with Celie, the confused Christian:

Dear Nettie,
    I don't write to God no more, I write to you.
    What happen to God? ast Shug.

Who that? I say.

She look at me serious.

Big a devil as you is, I say, you not worried bout no God, surely.

She say, Wait a minute. Hold on just a minute here. Just because I don't harass it like some peoples us know don't mean I ain't got religion.

What God do for me? I ast.

She say, Celie! Like she shock. He gave you life, good health, and a good woman that love you to death.

Yeah, I say, and he give me a lynched daddy, a crazy mama, a lowdown dog of a step pa and a sister I probably won't ever see again. Anyhow, I say, the God I been praying and writing to is a man. And act just like all the other mens I know. Trifling, forgitful and lowdown.

She say, Miss Celie. You better hush. God might hear you.

Let'im hear me, I say. If he ever listened to poor colored women the world would be a different place, I can tell you.

She talk and talk, trying to budge me way from blasphemy. But I blaspheme much as I want to.

All my life I never care what people thought bout nothing I did, I say. But deep in my heart I care about God. What he going to think. And come to find out, he don't think. Just sit up there glorying in being deef, I reckon. But it ain't easy trying to do without God. Even if you know he ain't there, trying to do without him is a strain.

I is a sinner, say Shug. Cause I was born. I don't deny it. But once you find out what's out there waiting for us, what else can you be?

Sinners have more good times, I say.

You know why? she ast.

Cause you ain't all the time worrying bout God, I say.

Naw, that ain't it, she say. Us worry bout God a lot. But once us feel loved by God, us do the best us can to please him with what us like.

You telling me God love you, and you ain't never done nothing for him? I mean, not go to church, sing in the choir, feed the preacher and all like that?

But if God love me, Celie, I don't have to do all that. Unless I want to. There's a lot of other things I can do that I speck God likes.

Like what? I ast.

Oh, she say. I can lay back and just admire stuff. Be happy. Have a good time.

Well, this sound like blasphemy sure nuff.

She say, Celie, tell the truth, have you ever found God in church? I never did. I just found a bunch of folks hoping for him to show. Any God I ever felt in church I brought in with me. And I think all the other folks did too. They come to church to share God, not find God.

Some folks didn't have him to share, I said. They the ones didn't speak to me while I was there struggling with my big belly and Mr. ———'s children.

Right, she say.

Then she say: Tell me what your God look like, Celie.

Aw naw, I say. I'm too shame. Nobody ever ast me this before, so I'm sort of took by surprise. Besides, when I think about it, it don't seem quite right. But it all I got. I decide to stick up for him, just to see what Shug say.

Okay, I say. He big and old and tall and graybearded and white. He wear white robes and go barefooted.

Blue eyes? she ast.

Sort of bluish-gray. Cool. Big though. White lashes, I say.

She laugh.

Why you laugh? I ast. I don't think it so funny. What you expect him to look like, Mr. ———?

That wouldn't be no improvement, she say. Then she tell me this old white man is the same God she used to see when she prayed. If you wait to find God in church, Celie, she say, that's who is bound to show up, cause that's where he live.

How come? I ast.

Cause that's the one that's in the white folks' white bible.

Shug! I say. God wrote the bible, white folks had nothing to do with it.

How come he look just like them, then? Only bigger? And a heap more hair. How come the bible just like everything else they make, all about them doing one thing and another, and all the colored folks doing is gitting cursed.

I never thought bout that.

Nettie say somewhere in the bible it say Jesus' hair was like lamb's wool, I say.

Well, say Shug, if he came to any of these churches we talking bout he'd have to have it conked before anybody paid him any attention. The last thing niggers want to think about they God is that his hair kinky.

That's the truth, I say.

Ain't no way to read the bible and not think God white, she say. Then she sigh. When I found out I thought God was white, and a man, I lost interest. You mad cause he don't seem to listen to your prayers. Humph! Do the mayor listen to anything colored say? Ask Sofia, she say.

But I don't have to ast Sofia. I know white people never listen to colored, period. If they do, they only listen long enought to be able to tell you what to do.

Here's the thing, say Shug. The thing I believe. God is inside you and inside everybody else. You come into the world with God. But only them that search for it inside find it. And sometimes it just manifest itself even if you not looking, or don't know what you looking for. Trouble do it for most folks, I think. Sorrow, lord. Feeling like shit.

It? I ast.

Yeah, It. God ain't a he or a she, but a It. Maybe a "us."

But what do it look like? I ast.

Don't look like nothing, she say. It ain't a picture show. It ain't something you can look at apart from anything else, including yourself. I believe God is everything, say Shug. Everything that is or ever was or ever will be. And when you can feel that, and be happy to feel that, you've found It.

Shug a beautiful something, let me tell you. She frown a little, look out cross the yard, lean back in her chair, look like a big rose.

She say, My first step from the old white man was trees. Then air. Then birds. Then other people. But one day when I was sitting quiet and feeling like a motherless child, which I was, it come to me: that feeling of being part of everything, not separate at all. I knew that if I cut a tree, my arm would bleed. And I laughed and I cried and I run all round the house. I knew just what it was. In fact, when it happen, you can't miss it. It sort of like you know what, she say, grinning, and rubbing high up on my thigh.

Shug! I say.

Oh, she say. God love all them feelings. That's some of the best stuff God did. And when you know God loves 'em you enjoys 'em a lot more. You can just relax, go with everything that's going, and praise God by liking what you like.

God don't think it dirty? I ast.

Naw, she say. God made it. Listen, God love everything you love—and a mess of stuff you don't. But more than anything else, God love admiration.

You saying God vain? I ast.

Naw, she say. Not vain, just wanting to share a good thing. I think it pisses God off if you walk by the color purple in a field somewhere and don't notice it.

What it do when it pissed off? I ast.

Oh, it make something else. People think pleasing God is all God care about. But any fool living in the world can see it always trying to please us back.

Yeah? I say.

Yeah, she say. It always making little surprises and springing them on us when us least suspect.

You mean it want to be loved, just like the bible say.

Yes, Celie, she say. Everything want to be loved. Us sing and dance, make faces and give flower bouquets, trying to be loved. You ever notice that trees do everything to get attention we do, except walk?

Well, us talk and talk bout God, but I'm still adrift. Trying to chase that old white man out of my head. I been so busy thinking bout him I never truly notice nothing God make. Not a blade of corn (how it do that?) not the color purple (where it come from?). Not the little wildflowers. Nothing.

Now that my eyes opening, I feels like a fool. Next to any little scrub of a bush in my yard, Mr. ———'s evil sort of shrink. But not altogether. Still, it is like Shug say, You have to git man off your eyeball, before you can see anything a'tall.

Man corrupt everything, say Shug. He on your box of grits, in your head, and all over the radio. He try to make you think he everywhere. Soon as you think he everywhere, you think he God. But he ain't. Whenever you trying to pray, and man plop himself on the other end of it, tell him to git lost, say Shug. Conjure up flowers, wind, water, a big rock.

But this hard work, let me tell you. He been there so long, he don't want to budge. He threaten lightning, floods and earthquakes. Us fight. I hardly pray at all. Every time I conjure up a rock, I throw it.

Amen

In day-to-day life, I worship the Earth as God—representing everything—and Nature as its spirit. But for a long time I was confused. After all, when someone you trust shows you a picture of a blond, blue-eyed Jesus Christ and tells you he's the son of God, you get an instant image of his father: an older version of him. When you're taught God loves you, but only if you're good, obedient, trusting, and so forth, and you know you're that way only some of the time, there's a tendency to deny your shadow side. Hence the hypocrisy I noted early on in our church.

The church I attended as a child still stands. It is small, almost tiny, and made of very old, silver-gray lumber, painted white a couple of decades ago, when an indoor toilet was also added. It is simple, serene, sweet. It used to nestle amid vivid green foliage at a curve in a sandy dirt road; inside, its rough-hewn benches smelled warmly of pine. Its yard was shaded by a huge red oak tree, from which people took bits of bark to brew a tonic for their chickens. I remember my mother boiling the bark she'd cut from the tree and feeding the reddish brown "tea" to her pullets, who, without it, were likely to cannibalize each other. The county, years later, and without warning, cut down the tree and straightened and paved the road. In an attempt to create a tourist industry where none had existed before, they flooded the surrounding countryside. The fisherpeople from far away who whiz by in their pickup trucks today know nothing about what they see. To us, they are so unconnected to the land they appear to hover above it, like ghosts.

The church was donated to our community in 1866, after the Emancipation Proclamation, by the daughter of the slaveowner. It is "ours" only for as long as services are held there. Few young people have remained interested in the church, and so it has been kept going by one or two elderly women. I have supported their effort to keep the church open by responding to whatever modest requests for assistance they have made. I do this because I respect these old women, and also because I recognize them as the keepers of a personal heritage that is very dear to me. The cemetery with virtually all of my relatives, including grandparents and parents, is just across the way, as is the vetch-covered space where the first consolidated school for black people in our community used to stand. A school my father was instrumental in erecting. I find myself once or twice a year sitting on the church steps, peeking into the windows, or just standing in the yard, remembering.

What I remember is playing tag and hide-and-go-seek with my cousin and best friend, Delilah.* She was radiantly black, funny, and

___

* Not her real name.

fleet of foot, and her mother dressed her in airy, colorful summer dresses and patent-leather shoes, just the way my mother dressed me. Perhaps she had more pigtails; I had bigger bows. In winter we wore identical maroon-colored snowsuits, which served us well in the uninsulated church, which was then, and still is, heated by a potbellied stove. We would grow up and lose touch, and she would barely escape a violently abusive marriage, about which I would hear only after the fact. I remember my father huddled with other men outside under the trees, laughing. My mother, scrubbed and shining, smiling. We were all on our best behavior; even my incorrigibly raucous brothers, who, only at church, managed to be both neat and quiet.

Because we were Methodists and sang mostly standard hymns, the singing wasn't all that great. I loved it, though, because I liked singing with others—still do—and I was, even as a small child, humbled by the sincerity in the voices of everyone. After we sang any kind of song together, there was nobody in the congregation I didn't love.

Perhaps the singing had been even more arresting a hundred years earlier; legend had it that the former slaveowners would stop their buggies underneath the red oak to listen. Sometimes professional gospel singers came down from Atlanta and "turned the place out." They were undisputed queens in their shiny red or blue robes: They shouted at God as if they knew Him personally and also knew He was hard of hearing. The black stuff around their eyes, which began to run and smear the moment they began to sweat, was strange to us, as was the fact that they wore, and wiped off, more lipstick in an afternoon than my plain, country-beauty mother would own in her life.

My mother, in addition to her other duties as worker, wife, and mother of eight children, was also mother of the church. I realize now that I was kind of a little church mother in training, as I set out for the church with her on Saturday mornings. We would mop the bare pine floors, run dust rags over the benches, and wash the windows. Take out the ashes, dump them behind the outhouse, clean the outhouse, and be sure there was adequate paper. We would sweep the carpeting around the pulpit and I would reverently dust off the Bible. Each Saturday my mother slipped a starched and ironed snowy-white doily underneath it.

One season she resolved to completely redo the pulpit area. With a hammer and tacks and rich, wine-dark cloth she'd managed to purchase from meager savings, she upholstered the chairs, including the thronelike one in which the preacher sat. She also laid new carpeting. On Sunday morning she would bring flowers from her garden.

There has never been anyone who amazed and delighted me as consistently as my mother did when I was a child. Part of her magic was her calm, no-nonsense manner. If it could be done, she could probably do it, was her attitude. She enjoyed being strong and capable. Anything she didn't know how to do, she could learn. I was thrilled to be her apprentice.

My father and brothers cleared the cemetery of brush and cut the grass around the church while we were inside. By the time we were finished, everything sparkled. We stood back and admired our work.

Sister Walker, my mother, was thanked for making the church so beautiful, but this wise woman, who knew so many things about life and the mysteries of the heart, the spirit, and the soul, was never asked to speak to the congregation. If she and other "mothers" and "sisters" of the church had been asked to speak, if it had been taken for granted that they had vision and insight to match their labor and their love, would the church be alive today?

And what would the women have said? Would they have protested that the Eve of the Bible did not represent them? That they had never been that curious? But of course they had been just as curious. If a tree had appeared in their midst with an attractive fruit on it, and furthermore one that they were informed would make them wise, they would have nibbled it. And what could be so wrong about that? Anyway, God had told Adam about the forbidden fruit; He hadn't said a word directly to Eve. And what kind of

God would be so cruel as to curse women and men forever for eating a piece of fruit, no matter how forbidden? Would they have said that Adam was a weak man who evaded personal responsibility for his actions? Would they have pointed out how quickly and obsequiously he turned in his wife to God, as if she had forced him to eat the fruit rather than simply offered him a bite? Would they have said Adam's behavior reminded them of a man who got a woman pregnant and then blamed the woman for tempting him to have intercourse, thereby placing all the blame on her? Would they have said that God was unfair? Well, He was white, His son was white, and it truly was a white man's world, as far as they could see.

Would they have spoken of the God they had found, not in the Bible, but in life, as they wrestled death while delivering babies, or as they worked almost beyond, and sometimes beyond, capacity in the white man's fields? I remember my mother telling me of a time when she was hugely pregnant and had an enormous field of cotton, twenty-five or thirty acres, to chop, that is, to thin and weed. Her older children were in school, from which she refused to take them, her youngest trailed behind her and fell asleep in the furrows. My father, who was laborer, dairyman, and chauffeur, had driven the bosslady to town. As my mother looked out over the immense acreage still to be covered, she felt so ill she could barely lift the hoe. Never had she felt so alone. Coming to the end of a row, she lay down under a tree and asked to die. Instead, she fell into a deep sleep, and when she awakened, she was fully restored. In fact, she felt wonderful, as if a healing breeze had touched her soul. She picked up the hoe and continued her work.

What God rescued my mother? Was it the God who said women deserved to suffer and were evil anyway, or was it the God of nonjudgmental Nature, calming and soothing her with the green coolness of the tree she slept under and the warm earth she lay upon? I try to imagine my mother and the other women calling on God as they gave birth, and I shudder at the image of Him they must have conjured. He was someone, after all, they had been taught, who said black people were cursed to be drawers of water and hewers of wood. That some people enslaved and abused others was taken for granted by Him. He ordered the killing of women and children, by the hundreds of thousands, if they were not of his chosen tribe. The women would have had to know how little they and their newborns really mattered, because they were female, poor, and black, like the accursed children of Hagar and of Ham, and they would have had to promise to be extra good, obedient, trusting, and so forth, to make up for it.

Life was so hard for my parents' generation that the subject of heaven was never distant from their thoughts. The preacher would gleefully, or so it seemed to me, run down all the trials and tribulations of an existence that ground us into dust, only to pull heaven out of the biblical hat at the last minute. I was intrigued. Where is heaven? I asked my parents. Who is going to be there? What about accommodations, and food? I was told what they sincerely believed: that heaven was in the sky, in space, as we would later describe it; that only the best people on earth would go there when they died. We'd all have couches to lounge on, great food to eat. Wonderful music, because all the angels played harp. It would be grand. Would there be any white people? Probably. Oh.

There was not one white person in the county that any black person felt comfortable with. And though there was a rumor that a good white woman, or man, had been observed sometime, somewhere, no one seemed to know this for a fact.

Now that there's been so much space travel and men have been on the moon, I wonder if preachers still preach about going to heaven, and whether it's the same place.

The truth was, we already lived in paradise but were worked too hard by the land-grabbers to enjoy it. This is what my mother, and perhaps the other women, knew, and this was one reason why they were not permitted to speak. They might have demanded that the men of the church notice Earth. Which always leads to revolution. In fact, everyone has known this for a very long time. For the other, more immediate and basic, reason my mother and the other women were not permitted to speak in church was that the Bible forbade it. And it is forbidden in the Bible because, in the Bible, men alone are sanctioned to own property, in this case, Earth itself. And woman herself *is* property, along with the asses, the oxen, and the sheep.

I can imagine some latter-day Jezebel in our community (Jezebel apparently practiced a Goddess-centered pagan religion, one of those the God of the Old Testament is always trying to wipe out) having the nerve to speak up about being silenced. And the smugness with which our uninspiring and indifferently trained minister, Reverend Whisby, might have directed her to a passage from the New Testament that is attributed to Saint Paul: "Let women keep silence in the churches." He would run his pudgy finger underneath the sentence, and she would read it and feel thoroughly put down. For God wrote the Bible, she would have been persuaded; and every word, even every word about murdering the suckling babies of your enemies and stealing all their worldly goods, was Truth.

I remember going with my mother to get water from the spring. What is a spring? many will ask, just as I did. It is a place in the earth where water just bubbles up, pure and sweet. You don't ask for it, you don't put it there. It simply appears. There was one down the hill from our house, in a quiet grove of trees. Someone years before had put a piece of a terra-cotta culvert around it, with a notch in the lip for overflow. We'd dip our battered aluminum buckets into the shallow well, always careful to spot where the crawfish might be hiding, and perhaps sit for a minute before trudging back up the hill. How on earth did the crawfish get in there? I'd ask. They are always in healthy springs, was the answer. Yes, but why? I don't know, that's just the way it is.

But why is that the way it is? Where did they come from? There were no other crawfish for miles around. I never saw them in the creek, for instance, where my brothers and I waded. This was a mystery that was not explained by my mother's final exasperated "God brought them."

I was happier with my father's explanation: "Well, you see, these crawfishes used to live over 'round Buckhead, but it just got too goldarn hot on account of all them fires the lumber company makes cleaning up the slag . . . so they held a crawfish convention, kinda like our revivals, and they resolved to move east. So they traveled and they traveled and one day they came to this place where there was this pretty little girl sitting looking down in the water. And you know crawfish love to be looked at, so . . ." In fact, neither of my parents knew how the crawfish got into the spring.

On the one hand, I could strain to imagine a large white man in a white robe—unfortunately, real-life white men in robes belonged to the Ku Klux Klan—lovingly carrying two tiny craw-fish down the hill to place them in our spring, or I could fantasize about the stouthearted crawfish pioneers leaving Buckhead with their Sears Roebuck catalog suitcases, crawfish-size.

The water we collected had many uses. We drank it; we washed dishes, clothes, and ourselves with it. We watered our livestock and my mother's vegetable and flower gardens.

Because of the criminal exploitation inherent in the sharecrop-ping system—in which the landowner controlled land, seeds, and tools, as well as records of account—sharecroppers were often worse off than slaves, which was the point. Sharecropping was the former slaveowners' revenge against black people for having attained their freedom. It is no wonder that under such complete subjugation and outright terrorism, which included rape, beatings, burnings, and being thrown off the land, along with the entrenched Southern custom of lynching, people like my parents sought succor from any God they were forced to have. The idea that as descendants of Africans and Native Americans and Euro-peans—Scottish and Irish—on both my mother's and my father's side, they might have had their own ancient Gods, or that as free human beings they might choose a God uniquely perceived by themselves, never entered their minds, except negatively. The "heathen" from whom they were descended knew nothing of sal-vation, they were warned in church, and any God except the one in the Bible was just another illusion produced by Satan, designed to keep them out of heaven. Satan: always described as evil; in color, black or red. African or Native American? Never admitted to be also a son of God, made also in the image of his creator, just the shadow side of him. And yet everyone in our family and in our church understood instinctively who Satan was. He was the other side of "the son of God" we always saw in the white people around us. Never did we see "Jesus" among those who insisted we worship him. Only Judas, and every day.

"Pagan" means "of the land, country dweller, peasant," all of which my family was. It also means a person whose primary spiritual relationship is with Nature and the Earth. And this, I could see, day to day, was true not only of me but of my parents; but there was no way to ritually express the magical intimacy we felt with Creation without being accused of, and ridiculed for, indulging in "heathenism," that other word for paganism. And Christianity, we were informed, had fought long and hard to deliver us from *that*. In fact, millions of people were broken, physically and spiritually, literally destroyed, for nearly two millennia, as the orthodox Christian Church "saved" them from their traditional worship of the Great Mystery they perceived in Nature.

In the Sixties many of us scared our parents profoundly when we showed up dressed in our "African" or "Native American" or "Celtic" clothes. We shocked them by wearing our hair in its ancient naturalness. They saw us turning back to something that they'd been taught to despise and that, by now, they actively feared. Many of our parents had been taught that the world was only two or three thousand years old, and that spiritually civilized life began with the birth of Jesus Christ. Their only hope of enjoying a better existence, after a lifetime of crushing toil and persistent abuse, was to be as much like the long-haired rabbi from a small Jewish sect in a far-off desert as possible; then, by the Grace of His father, who owned heaven, they might be admitted there, after death. It would be segregated, of course, who could imagine anything different? But perhaps Jesus Christ himself would be present, and would speak up on their behalf. After all, these were black people who were raised never to look a white person directly in the face.

I think now, and it hurts me to think it, of how tormented the true believers in our church must have been, wondering if, in heaven, Jesus Christ, a white man, the only good one besides Santa

Claus and Abraham Lincoln they'd ever heard of, would deign to sit near them.

On Saturday night everyone in my family bathed from head to toe, even though this meant half a day spent carrying pails of water up a steep hill. The water was heated in the big black washpot in the yard. On Sunday morning we rose, washed our faces, had a hearty breakfast, and went off to church. As the smallest, I was bathed by my mother, dressed by my mother, fed by my mother, and wedged into the front seat of our secondhand blue-and-cream Packard between my mother and my father. They had worked hard all week, for the landowner's benefit; this was their only time of pleasure, of rest, other than an occasional Saturday-night film at the local picture show. We spent most of the day in church, listening to the minister, who stood on the carpeting my mother had laid and read from the Bible I had dusted. Sometimes there were wonderful stories: Daniel in the Lion's Den. The Three Wise Men. David and Goliath. The Life of Christ. (Everybody loved Jesus Christ. We recognized him as one of us, but a rebel and revolutionary, consistently speaking up for the poor, the sick, and the discriminated-against, and going up against the bossmen: the orthodox Jewish religious leaders and rich men of his day. We knew that people who were really like Jesus were often lynched. I liked his gift for storytelling. I also loved that, after Moses and Joshua, he is the greatest magician in the Bible. He was also, I realized later, a fabulous masseur, healing by the power of touch and the laying-on of hands. Much later still I learned he could dance! This quote from the Acts of John, from the Gnostic Gospels, is worth remembering: "To the Universe belongs the dancer. He who does not dance does not know what happens. Now if you follow my dance, see yourself in me.") But basically, according to the Scriptures: We had sinned. (I did not know then that the root of the word "sin" means "to be.") Woman was the cause. All our life we must suffer just because we existed. Worthless, worthless us. Luckily enough, we would die, but only a very small number of us would get into heaven. There was hell, a pit of eternally burning fire, for the vast majority.

Where was hell? I wanted to know. Under the ground, I was informed. It was assumed most of the white people would be there, and therefore it would be more or less like here. Only fiery hot, hotter than the sun in the cotton field at midday. Nobody wanted to go there.

I had a problem with this doctrine at a very early age: I could not see how my parents had sinned. Each month my mother had what I would later recognize, because I unfortunately inherited it, as bad PMS. At those times her temper was terrible; the only safe thing was to stay out of her way. My father, slower to anger, was nonetheless a victim of sexist ideology learned from his father, the society, and the church, which meant I battled with him throughout childhood, until I left home for good at seventeen. But I did not see that they were evil, that they should be cursed because they were black, because my mother was a woman. They were as innocent as trees, I felt. And, at heart, generous and sweet. I resented the minister and the book he read from that implied they could be "saved" only by confessing their sin and accepting suffering and degradation as their due, just because a very long time ago, a snake had given a white woman an apple and she had eaten it and generously given a bite to her craven-hearted husband. This was insulting to the most drowsy intelligence, I thought. Noting that my exhausted father often napped while in church. But what could I do? I was three years old.

When I was in my thirties, I wrote this poem:

SUNDAY SCHOOL, CIRCA 1950

> "Who made you?" was always
> The question
> The answer was always
> "God."

Well, there we stood
Three feet high
Heads bowed
Leaning into
Bosoms.

Now
I no longer recall
The Catechism
Or brood on the Genesis
Of life
No.

I ponder the exchange
Itself
And salvage mostly
The leaning.

It is ironic, to say the least, that the very woman out of whose body I came, whose pillowy arms still held me, willingly indoctrinated me away from herself and the earth from which both of us received sustenance, and toward a frightful, jealous, cruel, murderous "God" of another race and tribe of people, and expected me to forget the very breasts that had fed me and that I still leaned against. But such is the power of centuries-old indoctrination.

We know now with what absolute heartlessness the male leaders of the orthodox Christian Church—not unlike those of orthodox Judaism and Islam—stamped out, generally after robbing them of their land and enslaving them, pagans and heathens, our ancestors and theirs, around the globe: a campaign of such unspeakable cruelty, which has lasted for so long, and which still continues, that few have had the heart to encounter it in art, politics, literature, or consciousness until the present era. If our awareness is beginning to change, it is thanks in large part to feminism and feminist scholarship, and to a resurgent belief in the sacredness of the feminine, which was deliberately erased, demonized, and disparaged in all major religions. But thanks also to indigenous peoples who, though a mere remnant of their former selves, before the invasions of conquerors professing Christianity, have risen up to speak in defense of the ancient Goddess/God of all pagans and heathens, Mother Earth.

In this connection, Haille Gerima's extraordinary film *Sankofa* has much to teach us. While being photographed, dancing and carefree, inside the walls of a "slave castle" in contemporary Africa, a black fashion model for a white, Western magazine finds herself trapped inside the castle's dungeon, from whose loading tunnels millions of enslaved Africans, from the fifteenth to the nineteenth century, began their soul-shattering journey to the New World. The woman is horrified to discover she has somehow slipped back into the past and is, in fact, one of her own enslaved ancestors. We follow her spiritual development as her own beliefs are denied her and the imprint of Christianity is literally beaten and branded into her flesh. People of color have been so successfully brainwashed to believe that white orthodox Christianity has given us something we didn't already have that we rarely think of what it has taken away. *Sankofa* speaks to this. It also, perhaps for the first time in cinema, graphically depicts the process by which sadists who purport to be Christians have forced their religious ideology on the cultures they destroyed.

In the black church we have loved and leaned on Moses, because he brought the enslaved Israelites out of Egypt. As enslaved and oppressed people, we have identified with him so completely that we have adopted his God. But here is another look at Moses, when God commanded him to make war against the Midianites, although his wife, Zipporah, was a Midianite, two of his children were Midianites, and his kindly father-in-law, Jethro, was also a Midianite.

From the Book of Numbers, Chapter 31:

> 9 And the children of Israel took all the women of Midian captives, and their little ones, and took the spoil of all their cattle, and all their flocks, and all their goods.

10 And they burnt all their cities wherein they dwelt, and all their goodly castles with fire. . . .

12 And they brought the captives, and the prey, and the spoil, unto Moses, and Eleazar the priest, and unto the congregation of the children of Israel, unto the camp at the plains of Moab, which are by Jordan near Jericho. . . .

14 And Moses was wroth with the officers of the host, with the captains over thousands, and captains over hundreds, which came from the battle.

15 And Moses said unto them, Have ye saved all the women alive? . . .

17 Now therefore kill every male among the little ones, and kill every woman that hath known man by lying with him.

18 But all the women children, that have not known a man by lying with him, keep alive for yourselves. . . .

25 And the Lord spake unto Moses, saying,

26 Take the sum of the prey that was taken, both of man and of beast, thou, and Eleazar the priest, and the chief fathers of the congregation: . . .

31 And Moses and Eleazar the priest did as the Lord commanded Moses.

32 And the booty, being the rest of the prey which the men of war had caught, was six hundred thousand and seventy thousand and five thousand sheep,

33 And threescore and twelve thousand beeves,

34 And threescore and one thousand asses,

35 And thirty and two thousand persons in all, of women that had not known man by lying with him.

These miserable, grieving, orphaned young women and children ended up as sex slaves, concubines, and drudges in the service of the soldiers and the priests.*

* In the discussion that follows I am indebted to the fabulous Elizabeth Cady Stanton, and her great work *The Original Feminist Attack on the Bible* (published as *The Woman's Bible*, 1895–98), for her insights and, more particularly, for her attitude.

Women have little voice in the Bible, and what voice they do have is given them only to illustrate the deviousness, silliness, untrustworthiness, and general insignificance of their sex. The only thing that makes them worthwhile is the birth of a son; they expend much of their energy trying to bring this about. In the whole of the Old Testament only Deborah, the judge; Vashti, the dignified wife of a foolish king; Esther, who saves her people; and Naomi and Ruth, the devoted mother- and daughter-in-law, stand out as women of substance. One cannot help but feel empathy for the Jewish women of the Bible, however, who had no rights under the law of Moses—and indeed were told to stand back when he came down from the mountain with the Ten Commandments, which, after all, were not written for them—and were forced to share their husbands and homes with strange, weeping women abducted from other lands.

As to why my mother and grandmother rarely spoke of their spiritual connection to the Universe, we have only to read these verses in Deuteronomy, Chapter 17:

> 2 If there be found among you . . . man or woman, that hath wrought wickedness in the sight of the Lord thy God, in transgressing his covenant,
> 3 And hath gone and served other gods, and worshipped them, either the sun, or moon, or any of the host of heaven, which I have not commanded; . . .
> 5 Then shalt thou bring forth that man or that woman . . . unto thy gates . . . and shalt stone them with stones, till they die.

This is a God who does not recognize you as His unless you are circumcised. I don't believe the men in the congregation I grew up in realized this; they were definitely not circumcised. On the other hand, reading the Old Testament, and noting how readily this God would kill you if you were uncircumcised (Zipporah, the non-Jewish wife of Moses, circumcises one of their "heathen" sons with a rock before entering Egypt), I am inclined to believe that the circumcision of women (genital mutilation)—women who wanted to belong, to be accepted by God—has some of its roots here. Certainly the slaughter of nine million "witches" over five centuries in Europe has its root in Leviticus, Chapter 20, Verse 27: "A man also or woman that hath a familiar spirit, or that is a wizard, shall surely be put to death: they shall stone them with stones: their blood shall be upon them."

Under this order the "wizards" Moses, Joshua, and Jesus—especially Jesus, who raised people from the dead and changed water to wine—would have been burned at the stake in the Europe of the fourteenth through the eighteenth century.

It is chilling to think that the same people who persecuted the wise women and men of Europe, its midwives and healers, then crossed the oceans to Africa and the Americas and tortured and enslaved, raped, impoverished, and eradicated the peaceful, Christ-like people they found. And that the blueprint from which they worked, and still work, was the Bible.

BAPTISM

> They dunked me in the creek;
> a tiny brooklet.
> Muddy, gooey with rotting leaves,
> a greenish mold floating;
> definable.
>
> For love it was. For love of God
> at seven. All in white.
> With God's mud ruining my snowy
> socks and his bullfrog spoors
> gluing up my face.

This is the poem of a seven-year-old pagan. The "God" of heaven that my parents and the church were asking me to accept obscured by the mud, leaves, rot, and bullfrog spoors of this world. How amazing this all is, I thought, entering the muddy creek. And how deeply did I love those who stood around, solemnly waiting to see my "saved" head reappear above the murky water. This experience of communal love and humble hope for my well-being was my reality of life on this planet. I was unable to send my mind off into space in search of a God who never noticed mud, leaves, or bullfrogs. Or the innocent hearts of my tender, loving people.

It is fatal to love a God who does not love you. A God specifically created to comfort, lead, advise, strengthen, and enlarge the tribal borders of someone else. We have been beggars at the table of a religion that sanctioned our destruction. Our own religions denied, forgotten; our own ancestral connections to All Creation something of which we are ashamed. I maintain that we are empty, lonely, without our pagan-heathen ancestors; that we must lively them up within ourselves, and begin to see them as whole and necessary and correct: their Earth-centered, female-reverencing religions, like their architecture, agriculture, and music, suited perfectly to the lives they led. And lead, those who are left, today. I further maintain that the Jesus most of us have been brought up to adore must be expanded to include the "wizard" and the dancer, and that when this is done, it becomes clear that he coexists quite easily with pagan indigenous peoples. Indeed, it was because the teachings of Jesus were already familiar to many of our ancestors, especially in the New World—they already practiced the love and sharing that he preached—that the Christian Church was able to make as many genuine converts to the Christian religion as it did.

All people deserve to worship a God who also worships them. A God that made them, and likes them. That is why Nature, Mother Earth, is such a good choice. Never will Nature require that you cut off some part of your body to please It; never will Mother Earth find anything wrong with your natural way. She made it, and She made it however it is so that you will be more comfortable as part of Her Creation, rather than less. Everyone deserves a God who adores our freedom: Nature would never advise us to do anything but be ourselves. Mother Earth will do all that She can to support our choices. Whatever they are. For they are of Her, and inherent in our creation is Her trust.

We are born knowing how to worship, just as we are born knowing how to laugh.

And what is the result of decolonizing the spirit? It is as if one truly does possess a third eye, and this eye opens. One begins to see the world from one's own point of view; to interact with it out of one's own conscience and heart. One's own "pagan" Earth spirit. We begin to flow, again, with and into the Universe. And out of this flowing comes the natural activism of wanting to survive, to be happy, to enjoy one another and Life, and to laugh. We begin to distinguish between the need, singly, to throw rocks at whatever is oppressing us, and the creative joy that arises when we bring our collective stones of resistance against injustice together. We begin to see that we must be loved very much by whatever Creation is, to find ourselves on this wonderful Earth. We begin to recognize our sweet, generously appointed place in the makeup of the Cosmos. We begin to feel glad, and grateful to be *here*.

This exploration of my own spiritual quest was presented at Auburn Theological Seminary, New York City, in April of 1995.

A contemporary "pagan" woman, whose home is the rain forest of West Africa. She is beautiful, self-sufficient, elegantly dressed, and serene, and the God/Goddess of Nature, which surrounds her and of which she is part, has obviously earned her complete trust. Only to enslave her spirit and body to the will of others need another God, foreign to her experience of Creation, be introduced.

PHOTO BY ELISABETH SUNDAY, 1989

PART TWO

Anything We Love Can Be Saved

Zora Neale Hurston on a folklore-collecting trip in the Thirties. Her foot rests on the running board of "Susie," her dauntless roadster.
PHOTOGRAPHER UNKNOWN

"You Have All Seen"

IF THE WOMEN OF THE WORLD WERE COMFORTABLE, THIS WOULD BE A COMFORTABLE WORLD

"You may touch them," he said.

I was looking at the scars that curved down his cheeks: pencil thin where they began beside his nose, wider—flat, shining—beside his lips.

Ever since we'd met at the airport in Accra I'd wanted to touch them.

With eagerness I raised my fingers to his face. In the mid-April heat of Northern Ghana I was surprised to find the skin of his face so cool. Gently I traced each scar—near his nose, finely puckered, near his lips, smooth as ice—with my fingers.

"How did it happen?" I asked.

"One day when I was a small boy—maybe five years old—my grandfather came to visit. As he sometimes did without asking my parents, he carried me home with him. While I was there, someone came to the house and did it. I bled a lot." He paused. "I also cried."

His name is Samuel Zan, and he is general secretary of Amnesty International in Ghana. Gentle in manner, reed thin, and very good-looking, he is dressed in a loosely fitting printed shirt of royal blue. It is the perfect color for him, the deep blue accentuating the richness of his very dark, luminous skin.

"Did it hurt very much?"

"Yes," he said. "It did. But it was the surprise of it, the betrayal, that hurt the most."

"I can still see it," I said. "The small boy's hurt surprise, in your eyes."

"My son looks at me fearfully sometimes, and asks if the same thing is going to happen to him. I tell him no. But he still has anxieties."

"It is probably no consolation," I say—what could be?—"but they are in fact beautiful."

"*Peaceful woman!*" he exclaims (the nickname he has given me), laughing in disbelief.

His scars *are* beautiful, because he is; it isn't even a paradox. I can hardly imagine his face without them. Which is not to say I am glad they are there. I place myself in the body of the small boy innocently visiting his grandfather. I imagine the harshness of being grabbed, commanded to be still. The scars are deep, not superficial. To struggle might mean a gaping hole beside one's nose, another mouth. Carved into his face to make him forever identifiable as a member of his tribe, the scars set him apart in the Western and westernized world; this too must be very painful.

This is a human-rights-awareness workshop in Bolgatanga, Northern Ghana, of African women and men who are dedicated to the abolition of female genital mutilation. It's theme: "Working Together for Change—Stop Female Genital Mutilation." It has been organized by Amnesty International under the direction of Angela Robson, a sensitive and dynamic woman from the London office, and Samuel Zan of Bolgatanga, and has attracted representatives from eight West African countries: Togo, Senegal, Benin, Ivory Coast, Nigeria, Sierra Leone, and Mali, as well as Ghana. The filmmaker Pratibha Parmar and I have come simply to be present at this historic occasion and to document, on video, the stories of many of those attending. We have also brought our film *Warrior Marks: Female Genital Mutilation and the Sexual Blinding of Women* to screen for the group. In this film I use the partial blinding I suffered as a child—when one of my brothers shot me in the eye with a pellet gun—as a metaphor for the sexual "blinding" caused by excision of the clitoris. Presenting my own suffering and psychic healing has been a powerful encouragement, I've found, to victims of mutilation who are ashamed or reluctant to speak of their struggle. Telling my own story in this context has also strengthened me, an unanticipated gift.

Both Pratibha and I are moved by Zan's story, for it links the suffering of small boys who are forced to endure facial scarring to that of small girls, who are sometimes scarred facially as well as genitally mutilated.

It is the story of his own birth, however, that explains Zan's vehement opposition to FGM.

"A brother died before me, being born," he tells the gathering. "My own birth was long, very complicated. It went on for three days. My mother suffered a lot and was never again really well. An odd sound came from her uterus from the day of my birth. Her labor was so agonizing that her cries attracted the whole village. It was a major ordeal. So much so that I was named to memorialize the horrible nature of the event. My tribal name means 'You Have All Seen'" (the complications caused by the practice of FGM). Zan pauses. "Implicit is the question 'What are you going to do about it?'" From what Zan is telling us, it sounds as though his mother was not only clitorally excised but infibulated (stitched shut) as well. This would mean an impossibly painful labor unless someone was there to properly open her up. Apparently no one was.

He retells this story to the camera while sitting under a mammoth tree outside the building where the workshop is held. I am asking questions, Pratibha is filming. In less than three days we have bonded. I feel I have known Zan all my life, and for many lifetimes before. I lean my head against his shoulder when he stops for breath. His lanky body relaxes in a sigh as he leans closer to my side. We shall probably never meet again, but there is definitely a forever feeling about the moment.

"Alice," he says after a long silence, "do you know what I believe? I believe that if the women of the world were comfortable, this would be a comfortable world."

For two days we listen to testimonies of adults who were overpowered as children and irreparably wounded. I notice that for some of the women speaking, it is as if a dam has burst. They tell their stories over and over, with the same stunned amazement that there is a circle of faces mirroring them. That they are being heard. That all of us have wounds, of one kind or another, to share. And that somehow making sense of our wounds transforms them. As with the scars on Zan's face, as each woman shares very private memories of a fateful day in childhood during which she was changed forever, I am overwhelmingly aware of triumphant grace, naked loveliness.

One of the more regal women telling her story is Madame Ba, of French-speaking Mali. Tall and stately, a magistrate in her native Bamako, each day she is dressed more elegantly than the last. Her story, it turns out, is not about her own mutilation but about that of her five daughters.

On the very first day we met, all of us, in the dusty garden of a guest house on the outskirts of Tamale, as we waited for our ride to Bolgatanga, she sat across from me and, through Yidu, a bilingual male FGM abolitionist from Togo, told what happened.

Her children had been mutilated against her will and theirs while their mother was away.

"*Five?*" I ask incredulously, thinking the number a mistranslation.

She repeats it. *Five.* Her eyes express sadness, shame, and a terrible guilt.

It is the family, she explains. Neither she nor her husband wanted their daughters circumcised, but they were helpless before the combined might of their extended clan.

Her daughters' aunts had the children mutilated, and presented them to her, harm already done, on her return home.

Hannah, from Sierra Leone, tells a similar tale. As a small, trusting child, she was cajoled into accepting a ride on an older woman's back, then dumped into the restraining arms of many women, who held her down as her clitoris was cut away.

As she speaks she relives the pain of the child she was; the adult woman disappears in the recovered terror of the child. I think of the hundred million or so stories still to be told, mirrored, heard. I can only hope the arms of the world will prove wide enough to embrace them all. But that we at the gathering embrace each other is clear from the beginning: Florence, just met, agrees to watch my bag as I search for a rest room in the Accra airport, and I, worried that she might not have eaten breakfast, and that there might not be food on the plane, bring her a sandwich.

The angriest woman at the gathering is also one of the youngest. She is the only one with a child, an infant boy, whom she breast-feeds while listening intently to what everyone says. Still holding her sleeping child, she rises to address us. The story she tells is of a young girl who refused to be circumcised, whose parents beat her and threw her out of the house, ending any and all support. She could no longer live at home, eat food at home, or wear clothing bought by her parents. She had to drop out of school because her school fees were no longer paid. She was forced to live with who-ever took her in. What, she now asks, do we think should be done to such parents?

Her pain and rage are palpable. There are many attempts to answer her, none of them satisfactory. Her blunt, courageous anger makes me think of Sojourner Truth baring her breasts to the jeers of white men at a nineteenth-century women's rights convention. It is she and her sisters, I feel, who will move the struggle against FGM ever forward.

In three days I feel close to Florence and Veronica from Ghana, to Caroline from Nigeria, to Blanche from Ivory Coast, to Hannah. When there is a break in the proceedings as we await the tardy male dignitaries who are scheduled to speak to us, we pile into Veronica's pickup truck and go downtown Bolgatanga—a triple row of shops and stalls—to shop. The truck is air-conditioned and Veronica has country-and-western music on the tapedeck. Gliding over the dusty, potholed streets in the white pickup, sealed off from the appalling heat as if in a Frigidaire, listening to a maudlin white man croon shallow love songs—to which Veronica nonetheless swoons—is a surreal experience of contemporary Africa.

Oddly, though, it is this stolen hour of shopping (I buy bottled water, a straw hat and bag) and love songs—a break we thoroughly enjoy—that pulls us through the oppressive heat of the long afternoon, when local chiefs, a government minister, and a judge have their say.

At first it is truly discouraging, being in a room filled predominantly with women, many of them wounded because they are women, looking up at the all-male bank of leaders assembled to address us. I feel I'm not alone in my momentary urge to throw something. The gender imbalance does not go unnoted: there is a collective sucking of teeth.

And yet, sitting at one end of the dais is the quiet, soft-spoken man who offered to help Pratibha and me with our luggage at the airport, and then out of thin air managed to bring us tea. I now learn he is a chief as well as an Amnesty International official. He is dressed like the party socialist he perhaps once was, in an olive-gray Mao-style suit that makes him look a bit Chinese. The day before I'd noticed him seriously cramming, with his head in the pages of the one copy of *Warrior Marks* (the book that chronicles the making of our film) available at the gathering, which is being passed from hand to hand, with obvious and heartwarming respect. I am soothed by his gentle presence and wry humor, and relax.

The evening before, over a meal of cold canned beans and gummy rice, I'd overheard him remonstrating with another of the male participants, who was trying to defend the practice of polygamy, which is rampant in Africa and results in innumerable hungry and destitute children, since each of an average of four wives (the number sanctioned by the prophet Muhammad) has children for a single "husband." I have been told the number of street children is increasing in Ghana at a phenomenal rate. In fact, I have been shocked by the scores of them I've seen. "According to this book I'm reading," the gentle chief had said, "polygamy is a forerunner of the plantation system! Instead of buying the women outright to work for you, you marry them!"

In the center of the long table is the major chief of the Northern Region of Ghana. He is a large man, forthright and jovial, dressed half in Ghanaian, half in Western, clothes. He jokes easily with Veronica, acting mistress of ceremonies: they apparently grew up in the same village and went to school together. He evokes laughter and applause when he bluntly asks: "If God in his goodness gave woman a clitoris, who are we to take it away?" He also calls circumcisers "butchers" and says they should all be put in jail.

Next, a judge from the high court painstakingly explains why the Ghanaian constitution does not guarantee the right to circumcise children, as some have apparently claimed, even though it emphasizes the need to uphold cultural traditions. Since the constitution stresses that the cultural traditions to be upheld must be "enjoyed," any ritual that causes pain is by its nature left out. He is followed by a government minister who calls the practice of FGM dangerous, evil, and a blight on the conscience of Africa.

It is a strong panel. Conscientious and clear. I feel relieved, though I personally believe it is retraining for gainful employment that the mostly female circumcisers need, not imprisonment. Pratibha looks over at me from where she's panning the audience. It means a lot to us to hear strong words against FGM from African men.

I have been disoriented by the long flight, the smothering heat, the food, and the challenging accommodations. Not to mention the depression I feel witnessing the widespread poverty and misery of Ghana, a country that, at the time it achieved its independence from Britain, in the late Fifties, showed so much promise. Hungry children, ragged adults, beggars, and hustlers are everywhere; the land itself seems under a blight. We have been told that the very climate has changed in the last several years, that the sun is hotter than it has been in anyone's lifetime, and that the misapplication of artificial fertilizer imported from the West has destroyed Ghana's most fertile areas. The combination of heat and chemical fertilizer has turned what was once verdant land into a desert. To be absorbed also is the meaning of the looming, malevolent slave "castles" we have visited in Cape Coast, through whose dungeons so many of our African ancestors passed. As well as the realization that the rain forest of Ghana—the "jungle" African Americans were taught to be thankful to have been delivered from, via enslavement—was destroyed, its trees cut down and shipped to Europe, long before saving the rain forest became an issue anywhere in the world. It has been difficult to sleep, thinking of all this, but also because of mosquitoes, unstable beds, and air conditioners that, when working, sound like trucks.

On the day that I'm to speak I am out under a tree interviewing Zan and have to be fetched. That I was chosen to speak on "Cultural and Modern Development in FGM" had completely slipped my mind. "Maybe it was the title," I say to the group. "I would never go near a subject as general as that!" Instead I talk about how, as a child, I became aware of violence against women. The group groans as one when I say that as a thirteen-year-old I saw the body of a woman whose husband had shot off half her face. I speak of my determination to remember her, to grow up and go to school and learn how to tell her story. How the indelible moment in which I saw she had newspaper stuck in a hole in her shoe was the moment when, just at puberty, I became a novelist. I talk about my mystification in Kenya, years later, when the subject of FGM was discussed among the people I was working with, building a school. I was by then twenty, but nothing in my own experience had prepared me to understand female genital mutilation. It took me years, I say, just to gather my nerve to attempt to write about it.

My presentation is followed by that of the Imam, spiritual leader of the region's Muslims. Slender and smiling, somewhat coy, he wears a white robe and flowing headdress. A necklace whose pendant is a lock of stringy blond hair of some kind hangs from his neck. He seems less sure than the other men that FGM should be abolished, though his presence means he is leaning in that direction. He tells a horrific story about the beginning of circumcision which he claims is written in the Muslim's "secret book."

In the Bible, he says, it is recognized as the story of Sarah and Hagar, Abraham's wife and his concubine. But in the "secret book" of the Muslims (not the Koran) there is a significant twist to the story. In the Bible, Sarah demands that Abraham banish Hagar and her son, Ishmael, to the wilderness, as Hagar's punishment for having a son by Abraham. But in the "secret book" of the Muslims Sarah deepens her revenge.

To atone for the sin of begetting a son by the unfortunate servant Hagar—and never mind that this was Sarah's idea, since she, at the time, could not become pregnant—Abraham offers to destroy Hagar's beauty. Traditionally, the Imam explains calmly, to destroy a woman's beauty you must cut her in three places. He raises his finger to his nose, then to each ear. But, he says, Sarah showed mercy to Hagar, and asked that she be circumcised, and instead of having her ears cut off, her ears were pierced. And, joked the Imam, Hagar could now wear gold earrings!

Traditionally, African women who are Christian identify with Hagar. I could feel this identification—a stunned, offended silence—in the room.

Until this moment I had been studying the Imam hopefully. Now I thought instead that perhaps this tale from the "secret book" of the Muslims explained not only the entrenched nature of genital mutilation in many Muslim cultures but also the original use of the chador, the black head-to-toe shroudlike garment that women in many Muslim cultures are still forced to wear. Especially the use of the veil.

Sitting in that bare, narrow room, on a broken chair that wobbled each time I moved, my brain steamed flat by the stifling heat of a part of the world I'd never thought of visiting before, I found myself transported back to my own childhood in Georgia, sitting on the creaking swing that graced our front porch, reading a comic book whose white male Western hero was enchanted by the seductive gaze of a young woman in purdah in whatever foreign land the action transpired. For days, months, years, this beautiful woman eludes him, until finally, one blessed day, worn down by his begging, she decides to believe he truly loves her and therefore agrees to remove her veil. He is shocked to discover that she has no nose, and that what is left of her face under the veil is covered with flies. Of course the Western would-be lover runs screaming back to his own culture, as I ran screaming to my mother. "What is leprosy?" I asked her, pointing at the word in the comic book. Together we looked it up in my dictionary. "A disease that eats away the body," we read.

But now I thought: They've lied about everything. Of course they've lied about the chador. Purdah. The veil. Perhaps it wasn't sickness or woman's seductive and evil visage the veil was intended to cover, but the marks of violence.

If you wanted to possess a beautiful woman, your fifth or sixth bride, for instance, and she refused you, or preferred another, or made faces and disgusted grunts and groans while being raped by you, or fought back, and if you, in a fit of rage, cut off her ears and her nose, as your "secret book" said you could, what then did you do? Especially if she had become the mother of your sons?

You insisted, I think, that she cover her wounds so that you would never have to see them. Or be reminded daily of her dislike of you and of what you had done in response. A thousand years later her descendant daughter would think it the female face itself that caused offense, not what had "traditionally" been done to it.

I was suddenly more grateful than ever that I had been able to attend this workshop on FGM. Otherwise I would have missed the Imam's chilling story, and this bit of the puzzle of the ancient oppression of women might have eluded me.

Response to our film—though sometimes hostile in the West—was, in this setting, among grassroots activists working to abolish the practice of FGM, overwhelmingly affirming. As was reaction to *Warrior Marks,* the book; a lone copy passed from hand to hand during the workshop, amid entreaties that we have it distributed widely in Africa—which would be a major feat, since there are no distribution networks in areas where genital mutilation is most widely established, and almost no publishing houses—and that it be translated into French (millions of mutilated women are French-speaking)—a lesser, but still formidable challenge.

Pratibha and I left the gathering feeling optimistic, nonetheless. A pan-African assault on the practice of FGM marks a major break with its past that Africa is poised to attempt. One that can only mean a strengthening of the African people and of the continent. The abolitionists at the workshop, women and men, struck us as uncommonly brave, trustworthy, dedicated, and sincere. We found ourselves feeling stronger in our own commitment to the health and happiness of children and women around the globe, and immensely heartened by the presence of the men who've come to join this particular struggle.

As we approach the millennium I think it is necessary to consider that the human race, like the living organisms that left the oceans for dry land, is at the beginning of learning an entirely new and different way to be on the planet. The way of *conscious* harmlessness. I view the commonplace, remarkably mindless attacks on the bodies of children and women everywhere in the world as a symptom of the race's collective madness, which stems, I think, from its insufficiently examined hatred of itself. A hatred that has never seemed to have sufficient cause, since so much hateful behavior, male to female, female to male, parent to child, humans to animals and the environment, has been cunningly hidden beneath the word "taboo," recorded, if at all, in "secret books" only a few male clergy could read. Ignorant of our true, rather than our imagined, glorified past, we have been plagued by an inexplicable anxiety, often violently expressed against ourselves.

But, as we have now all seen, mutilated women, in Africa and elsewhere, are increasingly mirroring a mutilated world. For the earth to know health and happiness, this violence against women must stop. We cannot care for the environment around us, our self-designated role from the beginning, if we are in excruciating pain.

Like Zan, I believe that if the women of the world were comfortable, so would the world be. In fact, I know this in my bones. Out of a woman's security—which always means free agency in society, sexual and spiritual autonomy, as well as the well-being of her children and the sanctity of her home—comes ultimate security for the world. Archaeological findings in ruins of matristic, prepatriarchal societies bear this out. Evidence shows that for thousands of years before male domination of Earth, women headed vibrant cultures that traded, reasoned, and celebrated with each other without the need to erect forts or walls.

Certainly the peacefulness Zan identified in me, a hard-won, not-every-minute-present peacefulness, to be sure, springs from my utter lack of interest in maiming, starving, killing, conquering, or otherwise inflicting humiliation and suffering on anyone or anything.

We will end the practice of female genital mutilation, and that of the facial scarring of children as well, because there are countless others in the world who also lack the impulse to harm, and who share instead the desire to cherish and to make whole. It will be a long struggle, waged neither with weapons nor words of blame, but rather with the understanding, patience, and commitment of a few thousand peaceful women—and men like Zan—who deeply respect women and love children, who are, after all, the ultimate foundation of a human future.

This conference took place in April of 1996.

*Alice Walker and Samuel Zan, at the foot of a large tree in
Bolgatanga, Northern Ghana. April, 1996.*
PHOTO BY PRATIBHA PARMAR

This photograph of an Indian man hugging a tree has been attached to my typing stand for years. Each day it reminds me that people everywhere know how to love. It gives me hope that when the time comes, each of us will know just exactly what is worth putting our arms around.

ROBERT A. HUTCHISON

Anything We Love Can Be Saved

THE RESURRECTION OF ZORA NEALE HURSTON AND HER WORK

*An address delivered at the First Annual
Zora Neale Hurston Festival, Eatonville, Florida,
January 26, 1990.*

Diamond Ash

My first visit to Eatonville was on August 15, 1973, seventeen years ago. I was twenty-eight, my daughter, Rebecca, three. Sometimes she tells me of the pain she felt in childhood because I was so often working and not to be distracted, or off on some mysterious pilgrimage, the importance of which, next to herself, she could not understand. This trip to Eatonville, not one of whose living inhabitants I knew, represented such a pilgrimage, one that my small, necessarily stoic child would have to wait years to comprehend.

But at the time, I felt there was no alternative. I had read Robert Hemenway's thoughtful and sensitive biography of Zora Neale Hurston, after loving and teaching her work for a number of years, and I could not bear that she did not have a known grave. After all, with her pen she had erected a monument to the African-American and African-AmerIndian common people both she and I are descended from. After reading Hurston, anyone coming to the United States would know exactly where to go to find the remains of the culture that kept Southern black people going through centuries of white oppression. They could find what was left of the music; they could find what was left of the speech; they could find what was left of the dancing (I remember wanting to shout with joy to see that Zora, in one of her books, mentioned the "moochie," a dance that scandalized—and titillated—the elders in my community when I was a very small child, and that I had never seen mentioned anywhere); they could find what was left of the work, the people's relationship to the earth and to animals; they could find what was left of the orchards, the gardens, and the fields; they could find what was left of the prayer.

I will never forget reading Zora and seeing for the first time, written down, the prayer that my father, and all the old elders before him, prayed in church. The one that thanked God that the cover on his bed the night before was not his winding sheet, nor his bed itself his cooling board. When I read this prayer, I saw again the deeply sincere praying face of my father, and relived my own awareness of his passion, his gratitude for life, and his humbleness.

Nor will I forget finding a character in Zora's work called Shug. It is what my "outside" grandmother, my grandfather's lover and mother of two of my aunts, was called. It is also the nickname of an aunt, Malsenior, for whom I was named. On any page in Zora's work I was likely to see something or someone I recognized; reading her tales of adventure and risk became an act of self-recognition and affirmation I'd experienced but rarely before.

Reading her, I saw for the first time my own specific culture, and recognized it as such, with its humor always striving to be equal to its pain, and I felt as if, indeed, I had been given a map that led to the remains of my literary country. The old country, as it were. Her characters spoke the language I'd heard the elders speaking all my life. Her work chronicled the behavior of the elders I'd witnessed. And she did not condescend to them, and she did not apologize for them, and she *was* them, delightedly.

It was very hot, my first visit to Eatonville. As hot in Florida as it had been in Jackson, Mississippi, which I'd left early that morning, and where my small daughter remained, in the care of her father and her preschool teacher, Mrs. Cornelius. I thought of Rebecca as Charlotte Hunt and I drove about Eatonville and, later, Fort Pierce on our mission. I wanted to mark Zora's grave so that one day all our daughters and sons would be able to locate the remains of a human mountain in Florida's and America's so frequently flat terrain.

Today, knowing as I do the vanity of stones, their true impermanence, the pyramids notwithstanding, I would perhaps do things differently, but at the time my passionately held intention to erect a reminder of a heroic life indicated the best that I knew. And we were successful, I think, Charlotte Hunt and I, for we lifted from ourselves the pall of embarrassment at our people's negligence. We acted for Zora, yes, but in a way that relieved us of the shame of inactivity. Paying homage to her, memorializing her light, her struggle, and her end, brought us peace.

At least it brought me peace. I should perhaps not attempt to speak for Charlotte, who volunteered to be guide and companion to me. And yet I felt that Charlotte, too, loved Zora's spirit and was no less concerned than I that her body not seem to have been thrown away.

But what is a dead body, what are bones, even of a loved one? If you mixed Zora's bones with those of Governor Bilbo, for many years an especially racist oppressor of black people in Mississippi and, psychologically, of the whole country, the untrained eye would not be able to tell them apart. And nature, in its wisdom, has made sure that the one thing required of all dead things is unfailingly accomplished. That requirement is that they return to the earth, which in fact, even as living bodies, they have never left. It matters little, therefore, where our bodies finally lie, and how or whether their resting places are marked—I speak now of the dead, not of the living, who have their own needs and project those onto the dead—for our ultimate end, blending with the matter of the earth, is inevitable and universal. I hope, myself, to become ash that is mixed with the decomposing richness of my compost heap, that

I may become flowers, trees, and vegetables. It would please me to present the perfect mystery of myself, prior to being consumed by whomever, or whatever, as rutabaga or carrot. Sunflower or pecan tree. Eggplant.

The spirit, too, if we are lucky, is sometimes ground to ash by the trials of life and tossed on the collective soul's compost heap. That is what has happened to what we have come to know as Zora. That is why we are here today, honoring her, startled, perhaps, by the degree of nourishment each of us has gained from her, startling in our diversity.

Zora Hurston's ash was diamond ash.

Diamonds, you know, start out as carbon, or coal, deep in the folds of the earth. Over eons enormous pressure builds up and crushes the coal into diamonds, the hardest crystals known. Then some of us, like Zora, are crushed further, by the lies of enemies and the envious hostility of friends, by injustice, poverty, and ill health, until all that is left is diamond ash. For many years now, thanks to Robert Hemenway, thanks to Mary Helen Washington, thanks to Charlotte Hunt, thanks to Sherley Anne Williams, thanks to feminist and womanist scholars around the world, and thanks to millions of readers, Zora's diamond ash, her spirit, has been blowing across the planet on the winds of our delight, our excitement, our love.

And this is only right; it is the universe's justice. And it proves something that I think many of us here very much needed to see proved, twenty-odd years ago, when the commonest response to a comment about Zora was the question Zora Who?: that love and justice and truth are the only monuments that generate ever-widening circles of energy and life. Love and justice and truth the only monuments that endure, though trashed and trampled, generation after generation. We have, together, accomplished the resurrection of Zora Neale Hurston and her splendid work, and can now tell our children what we have learned from this experience. Our children, who are by now grown up enough to fly off on mysterious pilgrimages of their own. We can say with conviction that anything they love can be sheltered by their love; anything they truly love can be saved. First in their own hearts, and then in the hearts of others. They have only to make their love inseparable from their belief. And both inseparable from hard work.

We can tell them that on the day that we love ourselves, and believe we deserve our own love, we become as free as any earth-beings can ever be. And that we begin to see that, though our forms may differ, as an oak tree differs from a pine, we are, in fact, the same. Zora is us. That is why, reading her, we smile or cry when she shows us our face.

I will close with this prayer Zora collected, perhaps hoping that when black people read it, it would evoke for them one of the most longed for and truest images not only of the African-American face but of the African-American psyche. For, like all spiritually authentic peoples, our ancestors understood that they did not need to be taught how to pray; that prayer, like poetry and music, of which it is mother, creates itself out of the lived experience, the pain and passion of the human heart. Typically, when poor black people sank to their knees, they created not a Lord's Prayer, but a People's Prayer.

I always weep when I read this, so bear with me.

> . . . You have been with me from the earliest rocking of
> my cradle up until this present moment.
> You know our hearts, our Father,
> And all de range of our deceitful minds.
> And if you find anything like sin lurking
> In and around our hearts,
> Ah ast you, my Father, and my wonder-workin' God,
> To pluck it out
> And cast it into de sea of fuhgitfulness,
> Where it will never rise to harm us in dis world
> Nor condemn us in de judgment.
> You heard me when Ah laid at hell's dark door
> With no weapon in my hand

And no God in my heart,
And cried for three long days and nights.
You heard me, Lawd,
And stooped so low
And snatched me from the hell
Of eternal death and damnation.
You cut loose my stammerin' tongue;
You established my feet on de rock of salvation
And yo' voice was heard in rumblin' judgment.
I thank Thee that my last night's sleepin' couch
Was not my coolin' board
And my cover
Was not my 'windin' sheet.
Speak to de sinner-man and bless 'im.
Touch all those
Who have been down to de doors of degradation.
Ketch de man dat's layin' in danger of consumin' fire;
And, Lawd,
When Ah kin pray no mo',
When Ah done drunk down de last cup of sorrow,
Look on me, yo' weak servant who feels de least of all.
'Point my soul a restin' place
Where Ah kin set down and praise yo' name forever
Is my prayer for Jesus' sake
Amen and thank God.

The Sound of Our Own Culture

Soul Nurture

My first Sweet Honey concert was in Washington, D.C., in the fall of 1978; an old friend and a great admirer of Sweet Honey invited me, saying she had something magnificent to share. I was not disappointed. Although I had heard Bernice Johnson Reagon sing years before as a member of the Freedom Singers, a group that grew out of the Civil Rights Movement of the early Sixties, I did not know what to expect, hearing her over a decade later as part of Sweet Honey, the vibrant group of women onstage before me.

Those of us who lived through the Civil Rights Movement and participated in those struggles can testify that, just as there were times when our spirits soared because of something we experienced by being with our people during a time of major transition—from servant to citizen—there were other times when, because of beatings, bombings, jailings, daily racist humiliations, the loss of loved ones, our hearts were nearly on the ground.

At the time of this particular concert I was just beginning to heal from the dissolution of an interracial, interfaith "Movement" marriage of ten years' duration. I felt my own heart had but a few inches to fall. It was a marriage that had had minimal support from our respective families and communities, yet it had miraculously sustained us through seven years in Mississippi, where my husband worked to desegregate Mississippi's schools and I worked part-time at various Movement tasks, from registering voters to teaching and creating history texts for the fledgling Head Start program. As time went on, however, it had become clear that my real reason for being in Mississippi, separated by one state from Georgia, where I was born, was to develop myself and my craft so that I might responsibly record, as a writer, the psychic layers of our people's experience at this time.

But where was I going now? Now that I no longer lived among our people in the South. No longer heard the soft, courteous cadence of their speech. No longer saw on a daily basis their bright, dark faces, so full of character, or could observe their sweetly determined, unhurried ways. Yes, as is obvious from this passage, I had fallen in love. What was I to do with it? In New York, where I now lived, I was, for the first time in my life, often afraid of other black people I encountered on the street. Never had I experienced such poverty, hopelessness, and hostile despair. Just this one reality, which perhaps seems commonplace now, was a staggering blow to my soul. In Georgia, where I had grown up, and in Mississippi, where I had lived, there were few black strangers whom I physically feared, so completely had the struggle against vicious white racism united us. It was a shock to gaze into the eyes of a black person on the street and to see myself reduced to the probable contents of my wallet.

And so I sat there, absorbing Sweet Honey's incredible beauty, a part of which was simply her existence, my heart slowly rising to the level of my lap as I heard "This Little Light of Mine," Fannie Lou Hamer's song, and then "We who believe in freedom cannot rest," a line from "Ella's Song." Ella Baker and Fannie Lou Hamer had struggled with us and for us to the very last breath of their lives; softhearted, strong-souled, willful, and heroic visionaries whose fidelity to black people and to freedom was a single unflagging beat. Now I could really look, through tears of remembrance, at the individual women who composed Sweet Honey. Except for Bernice, I did not know them. And yet, of course, I did. Before my eyes they metamorphosed into my grandmothers; all the way back to the African and the Cherokee; and my mothers, my sisters, my best friends, myself. And I thought: This is what's been missing. The absence of *this* sound in my life is why it is so hard of late to remember who I am, or what, indeed, the struggle now is. For what was I hearing, experiencing, taking into myself? Soul nurture. That infusion of spiritual carrots and spinach that one's own culture can give, and that the dominant culture under which we live cannot.

I thought, sitting there, of the word "culture." And because I am a gardener and grew up under the teachings of my mother, a gardener, and my father, a farmer, I considered what it means literally, in terms of health and growth. "Culture" is something in which one should thrive, the body and spirit simultaneously. But in the United States of America, for so many of our people, that is not happening. Instead, like plants whose roots are sunk in poisonous soil, we find ourselves producing generation after generation of blighted fruit. And why is this? It is because the dominant culture, whose values are designed to encourage the full development of the white and the male only, and not even of the disadvantaged in those categories, leaves the rest of us unsupported, except in ways that are frequently injurious to us. It is also because many of us have forgotten or can no longer recognize our own culture at its healthiest. We no longer know that *it* is the soil we need in order to survive, in order to thrive.

By the fifth song I knew why people travel hundreds of miles to attend a Sweet Honey concert. Why people get married to Sweet Honey's songs. Why people give birth with Sweet Honey's music blessing the delivery room. It is inoculation against poison, immunization against the disease of racist and sexist selfishness, envy, and greed. By now my heart had reached my solar plexus, and when I heard the old songs from my grandmother's Hardshell Baptist Church ring out as the freedom songs they always were, I heard all the connectedness that racist oppression and colonial destruction tried to keep hidden. I heard the African beat, yes, and all the African tones. But I also heard the Native American "off-the-note" harmony that used to raise the hair at the back of my neck when my grandmother moaned in church. I heard the white words of the old, nearly forgotten hymns, and felt how the irresistible need of black people to give contemporary witness to struggle infuses them with life.

These songs said: We do not come from people who have had nothing. We come, rather, from people who've had everything—except money, except political power, except freedom. They said: Yes, we were captured. They chained our grandmother to the mast of a ship that carried her away from every other face truly reflecting her own; her last view of home being, perhaps, that face, resembling her own, of the person counting the money from her sale. They said: Yes, they hanged your Indian grandfather from the tree beneath which he worshiped life. And, yes, the singers said, it is not over yet. For we are still captive! Look at the lies, the evasions, the distortions of truth, with which we live our lives.

Sitting there now, joined by the music with all my ancestors, feeling both my health and my wealth, I think: Yes. How sad it is for us that so often the only mirror we worship is the one in which we do not appear. Nor do we always recognize, with devotion, that which is before our very eyes. Why, for instance, does nobody remind us over and over again that Rosa Parks, the "mother" of the Civil Rights Movement, is as much Indian, and native to this continent, as she is African? And that there is a word, "African AmerIndian," that describes what many of us are? Why are we not constantly reminded, and do not constantly remind ourselves, that James Baldwin, who stood up for us so unflinchingly during the Civil Rights Movement, was a proud example of what a brilliant gay black brother/father/uncle/lover who loves us can be?

But now—there is a voice rising, clear and purposeful, from the collective throat of the group. It sings of Chile. It remembers Biko. It recalls Martin. It affirms love between women. It tells us we are wearing clothing that cost somebody's life. It warns us that the jobs we are often forced to take contaminate and destroy us. It tells us we do not own our children. It urges us to acknowledge the suffering, yes, but to savor the beauty of life, and the joy. Under this voice, the world begins to expand, and, paradoxically, to grow smaller. We stand on the shore, here in North America, a land that we love through great sadness and pain, and we gaze into the eyes and souls of folks we know in South Africa, Latin America, the Philippines, El Salvador, Israel, and Palestine.

We understand, at last, listening to Sweet Honey, what our freedom songs are for. They show us the way home, which is the whole earth.

My heart is by now in its rightful place, in proximity to my hands, which are made to reach out, as I write, to all those around me, the living and the ancestral dead, clarifying the struggle for myself, and perhaps as well for others. It is close, also, to my brain, which reminds me always to link, as Sweet Honey effortlessly does, intelligence—political and otherwise—to passion.

Sweet Honey is our connection to our roots, as well as strong branches sheltering, blessing, our connection to all who labor to create a healthy world. "Healthy" being another word for "just." This is a sacred role—this putting of the heart, the courage, the energy, back in our bodies. There is no way to adequately thank her for being this for us, except to live our culture, which nurtures us, which she so regally represents. And, with gratitude, to acknowledge it is the sight of our own souls' reflection that moves us so profoundly in her song.

How Long Shall They Torture Our Mothers?

THE TRIALS OF WINNIE MANDELA

The Stone We've Come to Throw

Winnie was asleep with her ten-year-old niece beside her. The child was staying with her for company, children being exempt from the ban on contact with Winnie at night. A light sleeper, Winnie was instantly awake when she heard a noise in her bedroom. Quietly, she reached out to the bedside lamp and switched it on, revealing three men in the room. One was holding a wire noose in his hand as he advanced toward the bed.

"I was determined that if I had to die, I was going to put up a fight and take one of them with me," says Winnie. She sprang out of bed, but a fight was averted by the piercing shrieks of her niece, loud enough to wake the neighbors.

Winnie phoned her lawyer and her vigilante friends, who discovered that the burglar bars on one of her windows had been sawed right through and then carefully replaced. They insisted she phone the police, which she did, though she knew it would be useless. "They took a statement and that was the end of the matter," says Winnie. "It is quite extraordinary how efficient the police are investigating other crimes, but no culprit has ever been brought to account for any of the offenses against me or my property: bombing; housebreaking; attempts at shooting, strangling, and stabbing me; damage to my house and possessions—all these have baffled the police. It is very strange that not one of the perpetrators of those crimes has ever been traced."

Several months ago I was invited to go to South Africa to cover the trial of Winnie Mandela, who is charged with kidnapping and assault with intent to do grievous bodily harm. Unable to attend the trial because of illness in my family, I have nonetheless followed it from many thousands of miles away.

The white South African court has charged that on December 29, 1988, Winnie Mandela and three codefendants, along with several members of the so-called Mandela United Football Club (a group of "internal refugees" to whom Winnie gave assistance and guidance, and who acted as an informal honor guard for her), kidnapped four young men, took them to the Mandela house in Soweto, and beat them savagely in an attempt to force a confession that they had been sexually abused by a white Methodist minister in whose home they were staying.

The youngest of the four, Stompei Moeketsi Seipei, age fourteen and suspected of being a former police informer, was subsequently found dead, with his throat cut. One of the members of the Football Club, Jerry Richardson, forty-one, has been tried and found guilty of murder. The three surviving men who claim to have been abducted claim also that Winnie Mandela administered some of the beatings they received, saying as she left them, "You are not fit to be alive."

Winnie Mandela, in a statement to the court quoted in *The New York Times,* February 12, 1991, says, "I did not take part in any assault on any person, nor was any assault committed in my presence."

She is also reported to have said that on December 29, 1988, when the men were allegedly taken to her house, she had driven to Brandfort—where she had spent many years as a banned and banished person during the late Seventies and early Eighties—to visit a friend; and that she did not return home until December 31. The men had claimed she met them at the door of her house when they arrived, wineglass in hand. (From this allegation, many journalists in the reports I have read have gone on to charge Winnie Mandela with alcoholism, falling-down drunkenness, and slurred speech.)

Though some members of the United Democratic Front went on television before the whole world and distanced themselves from her, the African National Congress is on record as saying that the trial of Winnie Mandela is "part of a pattern of harassment and persecution to which Comrade Winnie has been subjected for the last thirty years, both as a liberation activist in her own right and as the wife of our deputy president, Comrade Nelson Mandela." It has also considered the trial "blatant harassment of the ANC."

Nelson Mandela, who was himself incarcerated for twenty-seven and a half years for being a "terrorist" responsible for any number and variety of crimes, stood in firm solidarity with his wife, the mother of his children, and his comrade in arms (double entendre intended). "We have no hesitation whatsoever about asserting her innocence," he reportedly said, as each day brought a photograph of the couple bearing another assault on their privacy and human dignity, in what should have been months of rest and the rebuilding of a relationship irrevocably violated by the brutal activities of the South African state. Seeing them struggle, suffering still, hurts us; we who love them. And this is what is intended.

What to make of this, except to recognize that the courtroom and press, as instruments of a white-supremacist, fascist state, are merely the continuation of torture by other means. How is it possible that Winnie Mandela—after banishments, seventeen months spent mostly in solitary confinement (with a bright light kept burning night and day for two hundred days in her tiny cell, and without being permitted to bathe); after attempts on her life, the loss for long periods of her children, the absence of her husband, her exemplary work as a social worker who, from all accounts, seems always to have had a child in her arms; how is it possible, after the South African government has killed and maimed millions of children through starvation, lack of housing and medical care, and simply by shooting them down like rabbits in the streets or torturing them to death in detention—how is it possible that suddenly Winnie Mandela, and not, for instance, the notorious Security Police interrogator Swanepoel, is accused of harming a child? How is it possible that, although not one white person in South Africa has ever been executed for the murder of any black person, Winnie Mandela, who has spent her life feeding, clothing, and hugging black children, is accused and brought to trial for the kidnapping and abuse of a fourteen-year-old? If convicted, she might, "at the discretion of the judge, be sentenced to death."

I have been helped, in thinking about this case, by the knowledge of a similar one that occurred in the United States in 1948. The great writer Zora Neale Hurston—along with two other adults she had never seen before—was accused of sodomizing a ten-year-old boy. She would have been about Winnie's age, the mid-fifties. Though her case was thrown out of court—her passport proved she'd been in Honduras at the time of the alleged crime—the press (black and male in this instance) went to work on her anyway, quoting material from a character in one of her novels to "prove" she was guilty as charged.

Hurston, not having a Nelson Mandela or an ANC to stand up for her, and having alienated erstwhile friends by her "imperious," "flamboyant," and, to them, generally "uppity" behavior, attempted to bury herself in the backwoods of Florida, certain that her reputation was in ruins. She died there years later, never having known that a new generation of women would come along and recognize what she was capable of—not from court proceedings or newspapers but from the work she herself did in the world. A person's work is her only signature; we forget this at our peril. It is to the work and the life we must turn, especially in these days of assassination by newsprint.

It is Winnie's work—her care for children, women, the elderly, the "internal refugees," the homeless—that speaks for her. Her care for her own daughters, stepchildren, nieces, nephews, and, as a social worker, for the black South African family as a whole. It is the warmth and character and honesty that inform every line of Nancy Harrison's biography *Winnie Mandela,* and of the auto-biography *Part of My Soul Went with Him,* in which she documents the brutality of the South African government against her and the indigenous people of South Africa. It is in every thought she has expressed on television talk shows, to independent filmmakers who sought her out during her numerous bannings, and over the bodies of hundreds of slain children, women, and men above whose coffins she has been asked to speak.

It is a line from one of these speeches, in which she mentions "liberating South Africa with our matchboxes and our necklaces" (the practice of placing a gasoline-filled rubber tire around an informer's neck and setting it afire), that is used to give credibility to the image of her as brutal and violent. It is the image used as the basis for the frame-up.

She has not refuted the statement but claims it was taken out of context. It is interesting to note that others in the anti-apartheid movement, in moments of anger and grief, have, in their power-lessness, tossed out words of violence. Leah Tutu, for instance, the wife of Bishop Desmond Tutu, showed no compunction in stating to a television interviewer from *South Africa Now,* who queried her about the abuse and detainment by police of small children and the arrest of her son, that she was so angry that if she had possessed a hand grenade, she would have thrown it, she felt sure, blowing the police to bits. No one has, however, bombed a police station and accused Leah Tutu of providing the hand grenades and harming the inmates. Why?

Because the white South African government has come to know Winnie Mandela well through decades of spying, arrests, detention, and horrendous torture, and understands that, as Nelson Mandela's wife, she really is, as the black majority long ago spon-taneously labeled her, "the mother of the nation." In white lingo, "authentic first lady." They know that all their abuse has not destroyed her. They know she has always, characteristically, tried to "take one of them with her" whenever she has been attacked. White police, black and white spies and informers, warders, journalists, judges, recognize the fact that this lone black woman whom they have all persecuted so relentlessly may one day be in power, alongside her husband. They also suspect, correctly, I believe, that she is far more radical than her husband and has a longer and fuller memory of wrongs. They would like to be rid of her. They have tried, behind prison bars, to break her in private; they are now trying to break her publicly. If this fails, and her case is thrown out of court, as, in my opinion, it deserves to be, I do not doubt they will try to assassinate her, as has been tried in the past.

Whatever happens, as women, as black people, as comrades against oppression, we are blessed by the being of Winnie Mandela. Unlike so many of our sisters and brothers and fathers and mothers who died in detention under the boot of sadistic oppressors, Winnie Mandela survived to the point of total contact with the outside world, her life of struggle emblematic of what can be dared, challenged, achieved, endured, and overcome.

Reading through the sickening articles about her, in which she is condemned for the very enthusiasm, regality, and buoyancy of her personality and the styles of clothing she wears; roundly vilified for building a house commensurate with her years of hard work and her husband's stature as leader of millions (never is it mentioned that the house Nelson Mandel inhabited during his last months in prison, with its spacious bedrooms, living room, television room, and swimming pool, is *much* nicer than the cramped three-room "matchbox" with limited privacy and very little yard to which he returned); snidely envied for remaining beautiful, young-looking, and fresh, no matter what has been done to her (Nelson Mandela is now virtually "accused" of "falling in love with her all over again." The witch!); I was struck anew by the ease with which people believe the worst rather than the best about a person, even when the best has been a person's whole life.

Like Nelson Mandela, I do not doubt Winnie Mandela's word. Though one cannot, when she is angry and outraged, deny a glimpse of the Goddess Kali in her aspect, she is too much a warrior to stoop to ignoble battle against a defenseless fourteen-year-old. Too much a social worker to ignore screams she herself might have made under torture. Too much a neatnik and mother to have blood on her floors.

One friend I spoke to about the trial said to me: But, you know, she may well be guilty.

And I replied: Given the complete corruption of the white supremacist system in South Africa, how could anybody presume to judge?

But what if, on some other occasion, Winnie Mandela should fall from the obviously high standard of behavior she has always set herself, and should do something horrible and sad enough to make an earlier Winnie and the rest of us grieve?

Even in that case, ostracism, isolation, and prison would not be the answer, no more than they'd be if—in this interminable and bloody battle for our people's lives and dignity—she'd lost her hearing or her legs. As oppressed people, we ask a lot from people who stand up for us; however, a complete absence of mistakes, errors of judgment, or emotional and spiritual breakdowns should never be required. We have a duty also, I believe, to the people who forfeit their own happiness to hold high the standard of our integrity and Being. It is, at the least, to give a thought to the context of their actions, *to study them,* to have the humility to place gently at their feet the stone we've come to throw.

Songs, Flowers,
and Swords

Who Will Carry Any of Us?

In the summer of 1966 I left my job as a caseworker at the Welfare Department in New York City and went to offer my services, for as long as I could afford to do so, to the Civil Rights Movement in Mississippi. I was subsisting on savings and a small grant, which saw me through nearly two months of diverse Civil Rights work while attached to the Legal Defense Fund in Jackson, headed at that time by Marian Wright,* of whom I had heard.

On the afternoon I arrived in Jackson, I was taken to the local black restaurant and there saw for the first time the man I would marry. We did not speak. He was across the room with his colleagues—other law students like himself—and I was secretly hostile to whites in the Movement, though when we were introduced on a later occasion I managed to camouflage this, I think, quite well. In a very short time we were in love, with Mississippi as well as with each other, and after a year in New York while he finished

---

* Marian Wright Edelman, head of the Children's Defense Fund.

law school and I wrote essays and short stories, we were married (by a white Jewish woman judge who had married many interracial Movement couples, and to whom we presented a bouquet of pink tulips in token payment for her services) and moved back to Mississippi, in 1967, to work and live. Our daughter was born there in 1969, and with the exception of a year and a half she and I spent in Cambridge, we lived in Mississippi for seven years.

It was during this period that several of my earliest essays were written. What strikes me as I read them over is how deeply I was affected by my mother's life, and by one incident in particular: the story she told of the day she asked for government-sponsored food during the Depression and was denied it. The imagined scene of her humiliation reverberates through my work, as it has reverberated through my life. Indeed, it is quite ineradicable. That anyone could refuse my mother food sends me alternately into rage or despair, even today, when mothers all over the world are refused food or, worse, given (then sold) baby formula that kills their children, since it is often mixed with brackish, germ-infested water in villages where hygienic cooking conditions are unknown. But gradually I felt much more rage than despair, and that is what became more evident as I continued writing the essays.

That I am coming to take my mother's place—both darker and stronger—and I am accompanied by all the poor and dark mothers of the world, and we will not, finally, be denied—neither the food we need for our bodies nor the sustenance we need for our souls.

For though in the very early essays I appear to feel the world is mostly reserved for our "sons," "brothers," and "fathers," there begins the rising, effortlessly—because by its own earned force—of the dark women who become mothers and endless reflections of *my* mother. Mrs. Hudson writing her autobiography under a tree. Mrs. Hamer singing with sad eyes, but singing. All the anonymous quilters and flower growers I met during those hot days and fearful nights in the American South. Fighting Boss so-and-so . . . Fighting Miss Ann . . . Fighting the Klan . . .

The Klan again to be fought. Also nuclear power. Also prisons. Also lynching. Also, again, forever, it seems, the fight for land, for peace, for work. For a country in which our children may grow and not simply grow up.

I accept the criticism that I am trying to carry my mother, and that the weight is—heavy. Not "too heavy," as one woman has said. But who, I ask, will carry any of us if not we ourselves? No, nothing is heavier than this determination to affirm a mother the world despises. But at the same time, nothing is more joyous and more light. To watch my mother's smile as she reads *In Search of Our Mothers' Gardens* is to know true happiness. To know that she realizes I recognize and deeply value her worth. What prize, what praise, what criticism, can stand against this? This moment when mother and child look into each other's eyes and both can say: Yes, beloved, I understand.

That moment is the true beginning of adulthood for women, the true moment of rest and relinquishing of us by our mothers. For we have at last arrived at the place where they always stood: vengeful, harassed, irritable, odd, and we did not know why.

Many of my essays, those in *In Search* as well as those in this collection,* along with reviews and statements of various kinds, were written between novels and short stories and poems; before, during, and after a divorce; and while raising a child, for the most part, alone. The assumed support of a healthy women's movement is evident, I think, in the tone of many of them, particularly the dozen or more pieces that were published in *Ms.* magazine, where I was a fiction editor and then a contributing editor for many years. There is a story about the essay "Lulls" (published in *In Search*) that illustrates the importance to writers like me of a women's movement, and of publications both feminist and black.

Editors at *The New York Times* asked me to write a piece on Black America for the bicentennial issue of the *Times* magazine.

---

* "Songs, Flowers, and Swords" was written originally as an introduction to *Living by the Word,* an earlier collection of essays.

Rather, it became clear while I was writing it that they wanted it for the bicentennial issue. I had made a point of the fact that I was against involvement in this particular celebration, feeling how much of the status quo such celebration affirmed. In any case, I might have been talked into publishing the article in the bicentennial issue except for one thing: Over a very expensive lunch at Sardi's (where the bottle of wine cost thirty dollars), the two editors (white, middle-aged men) made clear in accepting the piece that they wished me to delete from my considerations of Black America my references to personal affection and sexual love. Leaving a one-sided expression mostly of fear, disappointment, and distress. *Their* view of Black America, not mine. Because to me, it is precisely our personal memories of joy and delight in each other and our present passions and loves that sustain us.

I was so angered I demanded the return of the piece and flew out of the restaurant in a rage (wishing terribly I had at least turned over the table and crashed the wine bottle against some handy object). And both *The Black Scholar* and *Ms.* published the article, as it stood.

The *Times* simply called on another black woman writer, who wrote them a better piece than they deserved. And I've often wondered if the editors who worked with her ever explained why they contacted her about the article so late. Probably not.

Having a receptive place to publish—not just the odd essay snatched back from the jaws of the *Times*—is of primary importance because it is so freeing. Though I've met many people, black and white, who criticize me for publishing in *Ms.* (others hate that I publish in *New Age, In These Times,* or *Mother Jones*), they somehow manage to ignore the fact that that is where they read me. What they don't realize is that some of the other publications they wish I would appear in have more than once received work from me that has been kept without comment (or payment) for over a year. Among other responses.

Someone has said that if I write about the birth of my child and I am not rhapsodic, this will hurt the child. Holding my daughter close to me, however, all I can promise her is not to lie. All I can claim to offer her truly is the example of my life. This is what I know. One's experience, in fact, is all one ever truly owns. If the essay "One Child of One's Own" (from *In Search of Our Mothers' Gardens*) is painful to her, I believe nonetheless it is better than a lie. Surely better than the lies I was told—"for my own good"—only to sniff them out eventually and become entangled in them.

We are, as women writers with children, in that marvelous spot of danger in which there is great risk but, as well, great possibilities for change. We can simply refuse to leave our children unarmed with the truth as we have experienced it. And that is my intention. Undertaken not with the arrogance of someone who possesses another (as yet another person has said) but with the humility of one who believes with all her soul that love is best expressed through truth.

Every one of these writings represents my struggle not simply to survive the past and remain nurtured by it but to embrace the present and fight for the future. In my mind I see us all quite clearly: poor and dark women, mothers in all the ways we are, marching with our songs, flowers, and (where necessary) swords.

PART THREE

What Can I Give My Daughters, Who Are Brave?

Rebecca Walker, Alice Walker, Bob Marley, Robert Allen, and Belvie Rooks. Dreaded friends and family. On a park bench in San Francisco, prior to celebrating Marley's birthday.

PHOTO BY HAPPY HYDER, FEBRUARY, 1986

Home

Fat, Balding, Rueful, Content

I divide my time between a venerable "painted lady" Victorian in San Francisco and a woodsy writing retreat in the hills of Mendocino. Because I've been happier in Northern California than in other places I've lived—Georgia, where I grew up, Boston, Mississippi, and New York—I've assumed this area is my definitive "home." It is, and it isn't. It has taken me several decades to understand why this is so.

When I went away to college in 1961, I left behind not only my aging parents but also much of my connection to my siblings. Because I was youngest, they left the nest before I did. One sister had become a university administrator, another a cosmetologist. One brother went into the Navy; a second joined the Marines. Two other brothers worked as mechanics; first in our small town, Eatonton, Georgia, and later in Boston, where they and their young families settled. My favorite brother, Jack,* invited me to live with his

* The names of family members in this essay have been changed to protect their privacy.

family during summers, where I baby-sat my infant nephew John-
nie or worked as a waitress or clerk. Staying at my brother's meant
I could save to go to college, an experience he firmly encouraged,
though it was one he, a young father of modest earnings, could not
have. His wife, Joy, and I were compatible from the start. After toil-
ing at our respective jobs all day, we had only to glimpse each other
to begin a merry evening of conversation, cooking, and eating,
while her adoring husband, my gruff but tenderhearted brother,
looked on. In fact, pleasure in his family characterized my brother's
demeanor. No matter how weary he was after a day underneath
broken-down cars, or fixing giant thousand-pound tires on the
frigid highways of New England, he came through the front door
beaming, happy to see his family, glad to be home.

It was his son Doug who told me, decades later, that his dad had
leukemia. All those years of fixing cars, inhaling gasoline, washing
the grease from his hands and arms with it. He also told me the
doctors gave his father little hope of recovery. My brother, however, sixty-one and young at heart, was determined to live. He had
consented to a challenging and high-risk chemotherapy treatment,
in lieu of a bone-marrow transplant. Not many patients survived it.
    They'd told Jack I wouldn't be coming, to give him the excite-
ment of a surprise. Poor thing, they said, she's in California, reeling
from earthquakes, fires, and storms. She's probably not stable
enough to send you a card! When I appeared, he was only mildly
surprised. He had believed I would come simply because he was in
danger, and his hello was sassy and assured. "How ya doin'?" he
asked. Then, as always, he said, "You look like a Georgia peach."
His lively eye and satisfied chuckle caught me off guard. He looked
anything but sick. Here he was, fat, balding, rueful, content. A Bud-
dha. Where was the man we all thought might die?
    While the chemo dripped into his veins and I massaged his
swollen legs, I witnessed and became part of something that felt
holy. From his hospital bed my brother responded with cheerful

good humor to an endless stream of people who came to sit with him. Old and young, all colors, men and women, children. All of them happy to be in his presence as he lectured his doctors about his treatment, kibitzed with his nurses, gave advice as needed on everything from marriage to baseball and divorce, commented on O. J. Simpson (innocent! he thought), the weather, world peace. Good-byes were reluctant, drawn-out affairs; no one ever seemed eager to leave his room.

I hadn't spent more than an hour alone with him in the decades since I used to live with his family during summers. My life as writer and activist, mother, and family rebel had taken me far away. Whenever I read my work in the Boston area, I invited him, and he appeared, his face glowing from the front row, but I was usually too pressed for time to follow him home. How good his life must have been to inspire the love I saw around him now, I thought, realizing I had been but one recipient of it.

During our take-away dinner I looked around me at my large and handsome family sprawled about my brother's bed, some of them relatives I rarely see, and then usually at funerals. There were brothers and a sister, grown-up nieces and nephews, hazily remembered cousins, and tiny tots darting about the floor. The harmony resulting from my brother's peacefulness prevented the small room from feeling crowded. As we sat there, eating and talking and watching figure skating on television—this was everybody's passion, and one I would not have guessed, never having sat with them this way before—a feeling of belonging, which I never experience in California, came over me. This is my family, and I love them, I thought. Really in amazement. After thirty years far from this familial coziness and my brother's undauntable spirit, I had come home.

My brother died on July 1, 1996, a year and a half later than expected.

Sunniness
and Shade

TWENTY-FIVE YEARS WITH THE WOMAN WHO MADE ME A MOTHER

Daughters Everywhere

First I see her smiling face as she stands at the gate to our house, waiting for me to open it. She has forgotten her key. I am always struck by her sunniness. It amused me many a gray day when she was an infant, and we lived in a dangerous and dreary Mississippi. There were glowing pussy willows outside her windows and bright posters on the walls; I awakened to the sound of her singing. When I poked my head into the vibrant room, she greeted me with a toothless grin. Today, at twenty-five, a sunny optimism is still her fundamental nature, though by now I have seen its other faces of sorrow, anger, cloud, and storm.

As soon as she walks through the door we embrace. She sighs, deeply, resting her head on my shoulder. I silently thank the Universe she has returned to me once again. I am always shocked she is so tall. My cheek lies just above her heart. I am reminded of her father; he is six feet. Of my parents, my mother, especially, whom Rebecca resembles, who was five feet seven. I often exclaim, "You are so tall!" She laughs. Kisses my forehead. "Mama," she says, indulgently. She doesn't bother to remind me I am short. For many years she did a curious little dance when we hugged, a kind of flapping of her knees against mine. It was uniquely Rebecca's, and endearing, if somewhat strange. She no longer does that, and I miss it. I think she dropped it while a student at Yale.

She has always been appreciative of our living spaces: as we walk from the front door through the parlors to the kitchen—in San Francisco—she notices every single thing. If there is a new painting, she stops to look at it. A piece of sculpture she'd forgotten, she's delighted to see it again. I love how observant and enthusiastic she is, for I know that, being this way, she will always enjoy life. As I put on the pot for tea, she moves about, touching, sniffing, exclaiming, and smiling; and I settle into a motherly busyness that expresses the pleasure I anticipate from my daughter's visit home.

Twenty-five years we've been together. One of my longest relationships, and the most important. As I pour our tea, I look at her and think: This completely separate person came out of my body; I have the stretch marks to prove it. I remember her turning in my womb, sucking her thumb, dragging a bedraggled pink blanket everywhere. Riding her first bicycle. At two she read her first word: "book." By the age of three she could pack her own suitcase. I see her flying out the door of our house in Jackson, Mississippi, a straw hat on her head, on her way to Jamaica with her father and me. I remember—a dozen or so years later, also in Jamaica—Rebecca lying injured in the middle of the highway, a victim of a motorcycle accident. I remember holding her broken foot, in the car, all the way back to our hotel, her teenage boyfriend, Brian, who traveled with us, glancing anxiously back at her from the front seat.

A bonus of being Rebecca's mother has been the love I've felt for each of her Significant Others.* There was Brian, a boy from the neighborhood, who was an early passion; Omari, a Kenyan

---

* Their names have been changed to protect their privacy.

from the island of Lamu, with whom Rebecca lived for several months, who used to call me in the middle of the night, when she was ill with malaria, to tell me not to worry; Bechét, the son of a friend, who seemed so much like my own child that when he and Rebecca separated, I was as sad as she was. At present there is Shawn, a smart and gentle woman who feels like a second daughter. This attachment to my daughter's partners surprised me; no one had warned me that when they suddenly disappeared from her life, they disappeared from mine. And that I would miss them. Or that, while they shared her life, I would feel I had two children to enjoy and worry over, not one.

I have loved being Rebecca's mom. There's no one I'd rather hear from, talk with, listen to. Except for those times when I've had to face the ways in which my being her mother made life harder for her. I believed the sunniness because it was real, but also because I thought it meant she was okay. Over a decade after her father and I separated, she confronted me with the hurt, confusion, deep sorrow, and depression she experienced, losing the safety and warmth of our marriage, intolerable for us but a sanctuary for her, and told me how she'd kept that side of herself hidden, especially her grief, for fear I would not be able to accept it. Accept her. My defense was that I had done the best I could, and that I refused to be judged. What she wanted, she said, was my simple acknowledgment, a *feeling* acknowledgment, of her suffering. I found this very hard, for it seemed to deny the difficulty of my life as her mother, and as a working, creative person, who had tried to do the best I could by both of us, sometimes under impossible circumstances and without support.

As a child, though my parents stayed together in a marriage that lasted over forty years and seemed to continue even after my father's death, I often felt abandoned, because both my parents worked. By the time I was ten, I was the family's housekeeper during the week, while my mother and sister worked in town; I felt like Cinderella as I attempted to care for a household that included a sexist father and brothers who were not taught to tolerate sensitivity. However, no matter how grim my existence was, I put on a cheerful face for my mother, whose exhausted face at the end of her day—cleaning another woman's house and caring for another woman's children—made me weep, inwardly, just to see her. Her place of solace and renewal was her garden, into which she retreated, leaving me with my fears and worries unheard, unexpressed. This behavior, I realized, had been reenacted by me and Rebecca, for when I became a mother battered by the outside world, my "garden" was my work. Having trouble dealing with Mississippi in the Sixties? Write your way out of it. The illusion I'd indulged was that because I'd married someone very unlike my father, and because I was a writer and not a laborer/housewife, and because I was an educated woman, and because Rebecca had been spared siblings, her experience as a child—I thought of her as extremely privileged—bore no resemblance to mine. I was so wrong. Behind the brave smiles she'd given me, during her years of sadness and feelings of abandonment, had slumped the little dejected girl I knew so well, twin to the one I had also been.

This realization catapulted me into a period of intense dreaming that led to partial recall of my own childhood—I had mercifully forgotten whole years of it—and culminated in a series of paintings (both savage and sad) that took me back to my anger. An anger well hidden by depression and thoughts of suicide. When I emerged, my heart broke open to my daughter's solitary suffering, locked in her shining, smiling ways.

"I did my best," I was finally able to say, "and still I hurt you. I am so sorry." My daughter is compassionate and forgiving. More than that, she is understanding. We sit, sipping our tea, and talk frankly about "the old days" of her growing up, my inadequate, perhaps, but still fierce-hearted mothering. Rebecca has made me a mother. Because of her I've reunited with banished bits of my own life; to know again the daughter and the mother I was, and to feel pity and empathy for both; to appreciate the admirable daughter courage that, though self-denying and therefore painful, still springs from a valiant solidarity with the mother who, in this world, always has too much to do and too few to help her. I've also discovered the world is full of mothers who've done their best and still hurt their daughters: that we have daughters everywhere.

Audre's Voice

You Thought Trees Were Green Clouds

The first time I heard Audre Lorde's voice was in the spring of 1973. I was living in Jackson, Mississippi. She called from New York to read a statement that she and Adrienne Rich were preparing for delivery on National Book Award night. All three of us had been nominated: Audre and I suspected the winner would be Adrienne—no black woman poet had ever been selected before—but I realized as we talked that Adrienne and Audre were friends and that they were determined not to have something so extraneous as an award come between them. I firmly supported this attitude. Audre and I went over the statement, the gist of which was that whoever was selected by the National Book Award Committee would accept the award in the names of the other two, as well as in the name of all women, those who would understand the significance of our statement and those who would not. Adrienne Rich did win, and she read our statement in her strong and brilliant voice, and to this day I feel this means we all won.

Many years later, a summer in the early Eighties, I heard Audre's voice again, this time in my small living room in San Francisco. She had been brought by Adrienne Rich and her partner, Michele Cliff, and while we chatted about the allure of the city, and how I had come to live there, Audre impressed me by her quiet scrutiny and detailed identification of the numerous rocks my daughter, Rebecca, and I had collected. What I didn't know at the time was that Audre had once taught at Tougaloo, a small black college in Mississippi where I had also taught, that we had both been interracially married, and that, like me, she had a daughter. (Audre had a son as well.) I was to find this out later, from reading her books. These were similarities—and of course we were both black women poets who loved rocks and books—that were never claimed and the possibility of a connection that was never explored. Was all this sheer coincidence or was there a deeper kinship than either of us, at the time, could recognize?

The third time I heard Audre's voice was in the late Eighties; I do not recall the season. I called her in St. Croix, where she was living after many years of treatment for cancer, to express my dismay at comments she had made about me in an interview. She had questioned my use of the word "womanist," in lieu of "black feminist," saying that it appeared to be an attempt to disclaim being feminist; she had mentioned as well that I had chosen to speak about the controversy surrounding the film *The Color Purple*—ongoing at the time—to a white audience, using a white medium. I pointed out to her that it is a necessary act of liberation to name oneself with words that fit; that this was a position her own work celebrated. As for *The Color Purple* event, I explained I had been interviewed by Barbara Christian, an African-American critic, on a hookup to dozens of universities and colleges across North America, some black, some racially mixed, some white. We talked until Audre seemed to understand my point about using the word "womanist": more room in it for changes, said I, sexual and otherwise. More reflective of black women's culture, especially Southern culture. As a woman of Caribbean heritage, she appreciated this point, I think. She hadn't actually seen *The Color Purple* broadcast herself but had relied on someone else's report about it. We ended our conversation amicably.

The fourth time I heard Audre's voice, in early summer of 1995, I was sitting beside Adrienne Rich at a screening in San Francisco of the wonderful and moving film about Audre's life, *A Litany for Survival,* directed by Michele Patterson. Adrienne and I had bumped into each other on the way to the theater, delighted and amazed that the three of us—Audre, Adrienne, and I—would be brought together once again. Audre's voice, rich and firm and true, filled the air. Her Amazon beauty glowed from the screen. Seeing her with her partner, Dr. Gloria Josephs, as they lived the serene and simple life of black women close to the edge of many things, including the Caribbean sea, was an experience of infinite meaning. I felt Audre's strength, and Dr. Josephs's, flowing into me. There was something timeless about them, a rightness that could not be overlooked or denied. These were women who loved women, loved each other, fought Audre's cancer together, enjoyed happy meals with friends, shared a coconut. You could see in them the ancient tradition of woman-loving being humbly and proudly carried on.

And for the last two days, as I write this in late summer of 1995, I have been listening to Audre again, reading from her work on tapes loaned me by a friend. As I listen, enthralled, I muse about why it might have bothered her that I prefer "womanist" to "black feminist." Or why she misunderstood my effort to reach out and connect with the many people who needed a dialogue about a film based on my book. I am glad that I called immediately after reading her comments and that we talked, sister to sister. I feel this more strongly than ever, listening to her now. For it is really an honor to feel accountable to Audre; to know that it matters deeply that we at least attempted to come to an understanding directly, between ourselves.

While I was meditating this morning, thinking of Audre's incredible legacy of courage and deep intelligence, I thought: She is clearly a fallen warrior. But immediately I thought: But how far can such a magnificent warrior fall? Not far, as we read in her books. Not far, as we hear in her voice on the numerous tapes she recorded. As she herself says about Malcolm X, I do not think I fully grasped her greatness while she lived, though I knew she was formidable. What I love about Audre Lorde is her political and emotional honesty, her passion for living life as herself, her understanding of what a privilege and joy this is. I love her patience, as she taught generations (by now) of women and men the sweet, if dangerous, fun of self-love. I love her cool stare back into the eyes of death, as cancer stalked her, and finally dragged her down.

I miss her. Listening to her voice makes me want to talk back to her. That is what I am doing here.

Audre, as I listen to you, and reread your books, I learn many new and endearing things about you: That until you were four, because your vision was poor and you didn't have glasses yet, you thought trees were green clouds. That the first woman with whom you made love didn't particularly appeal to you until you'd actually kissed her. That you sometimes thought of your white, Jewish husband as your third child. You are actually so much yourself, as you ramble the fields and corridors of your own unique life, you make me laugh, as anything that is original and spontaneous might. Once, when I was praising you, someone referred to you as a professional lesbian, because you always implacably presented that inseparable part of yourself. I was saddened by this attempt to minimize your bravery. I always saw your behavior, hiding nothing of importance, as the ultimate expression of dignity, and it is that word, along with others—determined, spirited, powerful, loving, and *grand*—with which, it seems to me, you are still only partially characterized.

Dreads

It Must Be Like the Mating of Lions

It has been over ten years since I last combed my hair. When I mention this, friends and family are sometimes scandalized. I am amused by their reaction. During the same ten years they've poured gallons of possibly carcinogenic "relaxer" chemicals on themselves, and their once proud, interestingly crinkled or kinky hair has been forced to lie flat as the slab over a grave. But I understand this, having for many years done the same thing myself.

Bob Marley is the person who taught me to trust the Universe enough to respect my hair; I don't even have to close my eyes to see him dancing his shamanic dance onstage, as he sang his "redemption songs" and consistently poured out his heart to us. If ever anyone truly loved us, it was Bob Marley, and much of that affirmation came out of the way he felt about himself. I remember the first time I saw pictures of Marley, and of that other amazing rebel, Peter Tosh. I couldn't imagine that those black ropes on their heads were hair. And then, because the songs they were singing meant the ropes had to be hair, natural hair to which nothing was added, not even a brushing, I realized they had managed to bring, or to reintroduce, a healthful new look, and way, to the world. I wondered what such hair felt like, smelled like. What a person dreamed about at night, with hair like that spread across the pillow. And, even more intriguing, what would it be like to make love to someone with hair on your head like that, and to be made love to by someone with hair on his or her head like that? It must be like the mating of lions, I thought. Aroused.

It wasn't until the filming of *The Color Purple* in 1985 that I got to explore someone's dreads. By then I had started "baby dreads" of my own, from tiny plaits, and had only blind faith that they'd grow eventually into proper locks. In the film there is a scene in which Sofia's sisters are packing up her things as she prepares to leave her trying-to-be-abusive husband, Harpo. All Sofia's "sisters" were large, good-looking local women ("location" was Monroe, North Carolina), and one of them was explaining why she had to wear a cap in the scene instead of the more acceptable-to-the-period head rag or straw hat. "I have too much hair," she said. "Besides, back then [the 1920s] nobody would have been wearing dreads." Saying this, she swept off her roomy cap, and a cascade of vigorous locks fell way down her back. From a downtrodden, hard-working Southern black woman she was transformed into a free Amazonian Goddess. I laughed in wonder at the transformation, my fingers instantly seeking her hair.

I then asked the question I would find so exasperating myself in years to come: How do you wash it?

She became very serious, as if about to divulge a major secret. "Well," she said, "I use something called shampoo, that you can buy at places like supermarkets and health food stores. I get into something called a shower, wet my hair, and rub this stuff all over it. I stand under the water and I scrub and scrub, working up a mighty lather. Then I rinse." She smiled, suddenly, and I realized how ridiculous my question was. Through the years I would find myself responding to people exactly as she had, delighting in their belated recognition that I am joking with them.

The texture of her hair was somehow both firm and soft, springy, with the clean, fresh scent of almonds. It was a warm black, and sunlight was caught in each kink and crinkle, so that up close there was a lot of purple and blue. I could feel how, miraculously, each lock wove itself into a flat or rounded pattern shortly after it left her scalp—a machine could not have done it with more precision—so that the "matting" I had assumed was characteristic of dreadlocks could more accurately be described as "knitting." How many black people had any idea that, left pretty much to itself, our hair would do this, I wondered. Not very many, I was sure. I had certainly been among the uninformed. It was a moment so satisfying, when I felt my faith in my desire to be natural was so well deserved, that it is not an exaggeration to say I was, in a way, made happy forever. After all, if this major mystery could be discovered right on top of one's head, I thought, what other wonders might not be experienced in the Universe's exuberant, inexhaustible store?

My Face
to the Light

THOUGHTS ABOUT CHRISTMAS

Seed Catalogs like Paper Flowers

I did not know what Christmas was until I moved to the West Coast. During much of my adult life I'd viewed it as a season marked by the ritual killing of millions of trees, just as, for me, Thanksgiving is a day that represents the ritual killing, and eating, of millions of birds. I was sickened by the thought of all those stumps, all those bleeding necks, and by the message given to children that it is okay to sacrifice living beings in order to express appreciation for being alive yourself, or in order to celebrate the birth of a sacred person, Jesus Christ, who was himself against killing.

As a child I had not thought of this at all. Then, the message was entirely different. I grew up in a historically oppressed (racially), economically poor, rural black Southern community where Christmas was the only time it was possible to collectively celebrate the only generous and cheerful white man anyone in the community was ever likely to know: Santa Claus. This was done with such enthusiasm and tenderness—and Santa's rosy cheeks were described with such bemused accuracy—that as a three-year-old one Christmas morning, I announced I'd actually seen him the night before, as he stole about the house, sampling the pies and cakes my mother always made and left out for him, and filling our shoeboxes and brown paper bags with apples, raisins, oranges, and nuts. (What would have been the imprint on white children's minds, I was later to wonder, if once a year they were encouraged to welcome a stealthily moving large black man into their sleeping houses in the middle of the night?)

When I became a student in college and studied the oppression of black people by white ones, and by the laws of white supremacy that still obtained in the South (so that as a child I could not enter a "public" restaurant, library, or swimming pool), I was angry with my parents for their Santa Claus worship. Until I realized that, like the white figure of Christ, whom they also appeared to worship, Santa Claus represented an ideal person who was *compelled* to be white (in a society in which the country's president, the mayors of towns, and the police were also white), and that their intention in accepting him was to help us all remember that there could indeed *be* an ideal white man, worthy of friendliness and tender regard (in a setting where not one white man was known to fit Santa's merry, adventuresome, and undiscriminating description). It was their desire to instill in us, amid the racist violence of the segregated American South, as perhaps it is the desire of black parents today to instill in their children in the apartheid violence of South Africa, a degree of faith in the miracles that one can expect to occur in human nature per se: a degree of hope.

But when I moved to Northern California I left behind all I had known about Christmas, and against the hectic shopping days that Christmas has become for so many, I barricaded myself. Going to the beach, reading, taking long walks, eating at Chinese or Thai restaurants on Christmas Day, or fasting on fruit. And then, because of the person with whom I share many of life's rituals (and a good number of its trials), I discovered what Christmas is. That it is the day of the winter solstice and was originally celebrated on the twenty-first or twenty-second of December, the day when the sun, having gone as far south as it ever gets, begins to move back north. It is, my friend said, the day the sun, the light, begins to come back in the Northern Hemisphere. In a way you could say it is the first day spring becomes possible. The birth of Jesus has been affixed to the seeming rebirth of the sun, but the rebirth of the sun has been worshiped since many millennia before Christ. Undoubtedly it has been worshiped, by plants and single-cell animals, since the very beginning of the planet's life.

This changed forever how I feel about Christmas. And how I celebrate it—usually, these days, with a sweat (via sauna), a vegetarian feast, and music making and dancing, with friends. I would never dream of killing anything for it; or even of thinking of it as an event that requires the least bit of frantic activity. For me, the excitement about the sun's return begins to build several days in advance of the winter solstice, and my celebration consists of a heightened awareness of the losing ground of winter, no matter how cold the days might be, and an intense expectation of the day itself, which, when it arrives, is greeted by my face turned up to the (if I am lucky) sunny heavens. The days after are spent in quiet appreciation of the possibility of another spring (my favorite of all seasons) and thoughts of seeds and planting. I lie late in bed, thinking of the sun as of a long-traveling friend who is at last coming back home to me, my collection of seed catalogs covering me like paper flowers.

It isn't that I don't think of Christmas at all anymore as a possible birthday for Jesus Christ (though it's true that I never think of Santa Claus, faith in whom, it seems to me, has been perhaps permanently lost), but I think of it more as the *re*birthday of every being that longs for the return of the warmth of the sun and loves the light. Surely it is my rebirthday too.

What Can I Give My Daughters, Who Are Brave?

This speech was delivered at Spelman College on Commencement Day, May 22, 1995.

A Woman Is Not a Potted Plant

While thinking of you, and of this special, blessed day—this day when you embark on yet another journey in your life; this day when you say good-bye to so much that is known, in order to embrace the much larger Universe of what is not known—I was thinking of the famous anthology *All the Women Are White, All the Blacks Are Men, But Some of Us Are Brave,* edited by Gloria Hull, Patricia Bell Scott, and Barbara Smith.

Brave. That's you. I look out at you now and I see it clearly. Brave is simply your name. I see the hope, the optimism, the joy, on your beautiful shining faces, and I know exactly what you are bringing out into this very scary world: you are bringing bright and willing minds, and strong and capable hearts and hands. The world, in its suffering and confusion, needs you desperately.

But what can I give you, on such a special day? I have stayed awake in the night asking myself this. At last it came to me. I can offer you the gift of my experience in many areas of life, in the thirty years since I left Spelman. I can honor my role as mentor, big sister, aunt, or even mother. Because, after all, you are all daughters of my heart.

My years since leaving Spelman have been rich in experiences of all kinds: in creativity, in struggle, in suffering, in growth, in evolution and change. The poet in me has made good use of everything, and as I look back, the poems are like glistening stones along the moist riverbank of trial and error I have walked along. It is the benefit of distilled experience you must have. It is the essence, the poem of my experience, that you deserve as medicine for your own journeys.

And I ask myself:

What can I give you for comfort on those bleak days to come— and they will—when you are wondering if "this" (whatever the limit is that you have reached) is all there is. I can give you this poem:

EXPECT NOTHING

Expect nothing. Live frugally
on surprise.
Become a stranger
To need of pity
Or, if compassion be freely
Given out
Take only enough
Stop short of urge to plead
Then purge away the need.

Wish for nothing larger
Than your own small heart
Or greater than a star;
Tame wild disappointment
With caress
Unmoved and cold
Make of it a parka
For your soul.

Discover the reason why
So tiny human giant
Exists at all.

> So scared unwise
> But expect nothing. Live frugally
> on surprise.

What can I give you for a day when the inequality of the world strikes you as so blatant that you are at a loss for words? When you weep instead of speak? When the scenes on your television and in your town cause you to feel some people are wearing generations of the suffering of others dangling from their ears and throats? I can give you this poem:

THE DIAMONDS ON LIZ'S BOSOM

> The diamonds on Liz's bosom
> are not as bright
> as his eyes
> the morning they took him
> to work in the mines.
> The rubies in Nancy's
> jewel box (Oh, how Ronald loves red!)
> not as vivid
> as the despair
> in his children's
> frowns.
> Oh, those Africans!
>
> Everywhere you look
> they're bleeding
> and crying
> Crying and bleeding
> on some of the whitest necks
> in your town.

What can I give you to remind you that each one of us constantly makes and remakes the world? And that if we can only trust in our own willingness to change, we need not despair? I give you this poem:

WE ALONE

We alone can devalue gold
by not caring
if it falls or rises
in the marketplace.
Wherever there is gold
there is a chain, you know,
and if your chain
is gold
so much the worse
for you.

Feathers, shells,
and sea-shaped stones
are all as rare.

This could be our revolution:
To love what is plentiful
as much as
what is scarce.

What can I give you to help you stay strong when you feel that
the world is turned against you and that you are standing, perhaps
even naked, absolutely all alone? I give you this poem:

BE NOBODY'S DARLING

Be nobody's darling;
Be an outcast.
Take the contradictions
Of your life
And wrap around
You like a shawl,
To parry stones
To keep you warm.

Watch the people succumb
To madness

With ample cheer
Let them look askance at you
And you askance reply.

Be an outcast;
Be pleased to walk alone
(Uncool)
Or line the crowded
Riverbeds
With other impetuous
Fools.

Make a merry gathering
On the bank
Where thousands perished
For brave hurt words
They said.

But
Be nobody's darling;
Be an outcast.
Qualified to live
Among your dead.

What can I give you to help you through the day, which will
surely come, when you give your glowing heart to someone
unworthy of it? I give you this poem:

NEVER OFFER YOUR HEART
TO SOMEONE WHO EATS HEARTS

Never offer your heart
to someone who eats hearts
who finds heartmeat
delicious
but not rare
who sucks the juices
drop by drop

and bloody-chinned
grins
like a God.

Never offer your heart
to a heart gravy lover.
Your stewed, overseasoned
heart consumed
he will sop up your grief
with bread
and send it shuttling
from side to side
in his mouth
like bubblegum.

If you find yourself
in love
with a person
who eats hearts
these things
you must do:

Freeze your heart
immediately.
Let him—next time
he examines your chest—
find your heart cold
flinty and unappetizing.

Refrain from kissing
lest he in revenge
dampen the spark
in your soul.

Now,
sail away to Africa
where holy women

await you
on the shore—
long having practiced the art
of replacing hearts
with God
and Song.

And what can I give you for that day, which shall come without
fail, when you love and are loved by "the wrong person"? The person all of society deems unsuitable. But rather than honestly stating
its prejudices, it says instead that Love itself, and particularly the
fierce, heartbeat-accelerating love you are experiencing, is wrong.
Or, at the very least, out of style.

I give you: "While Love Is Unfashionable" (which I wrote for
the "unsuitable" person I married many years ago—who was simply the sweetest, bravest person around). And although this union
did not last forever, I have no regrets. Rather, I have a beautiful
daughter and memories of uniting in love and faith with her father
against the grinding humiliation of daily racist oppression in the
Deep South.

WHILE LOVE IS
UNFASHIONABLE

While love is unfashionable
let us live
unfashionably.
Seeing the world
a complex ball
in small hands.
Love our blackest garment.
Let us be poor
in all but truth, and courage
handed down
by the old
spirits.

Let us be intimate with
ancestral ghosts
and music
of the undead.

While love is dangerous
let us walk bareheaded
beside the Great River.
Let us gather blossoms
under fire.

Besides, in another poem about love, "Beyond What," I can tell
you:

We reach for destinies beyond
what we have come to know
and in the romantic hush
of promises
perceive each
the other's life
as known mystery.
Shared. But inviolate.
No melting. No squeezing
into One.
We swing our eyes around
as well as side to side
to see the world.

To choose, renounce,
this, or that—
call it a council between equals
call it love.

And what can I give you for the day when you realize you don't
know what you're doing or where you're going? A day that will
come, as surely as the night follows the day. A day when you've lost

your way, your light, your joy, and maybe even your self. A day, in fact, when all you have are questions, not one single answer, and these questions feel like a nest of snakes slithering back and forth through your brain.

I give you:

REASSURANCE

I must love the questions
themselves
as Rilke said
like locked rooms
full of treasure
to which my blind
and groping key
does not yet fit.

and await the answers
as unsealed
letters
mailed with dubious intent
and written in a very foreign
tongue.

and in the hourly making
of myself
no thought of Time
to force, to squeeze
the space
I grow into.

And what can I give you for that early morning hour when you come face-to-face with the realization that torture, in this world, is simply a fact of life? That if you look closely even in your own life, you can see its marks. Because, though your body may have been spared, one psyche is shared by the body of the world and it is the world's soul that has suffered damage, and suffers it daily.

I give you:

TORTURE

When they torture your mother
plant a tree
When they torture your father
plant a tree
When they torture your brother
and your sister
plant a tree
When they assassinate
your leaders
and lovers
plant a tree
When they torture you
too bad
to talk
plant a tree.

When they begin to torture
the trees
and cut down the forest
they have made,
start another.

And what can I give you to meet the challenge of the great pain
that is sometimes the result of telling one's truth to a world unused
to hearing it?
I give you:

CONFESSION

All winter long
I've borne the knife that presses
without ceasing
against my heart.

Despising lies
I have told everyone
the truth:
Truth is killing me.

I give you:

ON STRIPPING BARK
FROM MYSELF
(for Jane, who said trees die from it)

Because women are expected to keep silent about
their close escapes I will not keep silent
and if I am destroyed (naked tree!) someone will
please
mark the spot
where I fall and know I could not live
silent in my own lies
hearing their "how *nice* she is!"
whose adoration of the retouched image
I so despise.

No. I am finished with living
for what my mother believes
for what my brother and father defend
for what my lover elevates
for what my sister, blushing, denies or rushes
to embrace.

I find my own
small person
a standing self
against the world
an equality of wills
I have lived to understand.

Besides:

My struggle was always against
an inner darkness: I carry within myself
the only known keys
to my death—to unlock life, or close it shut
forever. A woman who loves wood grains, the color
yellow
and the sun, I am happy to fight
all outside murderers
as I see I must.

What can I give you to help you embrace the Black and the
Red and the White in you? To help you know this fusion is a
source not of disgrace but of lived presence in the history of our
troubled country? A source of strength, and also of humor?

I offer you:

SOME THINGS I LIKE
ABOUT MY TRIPLE BLOODS
(The African, the European, and the Cherokee)

Black relatives
you are always
putting yourselves
down
But you almost never
put down
Africa
You are the last
man
woman
and child
to stand up
for everybody's
Mother
(though so much rampant motherfuckering in the language
makes one

blue)
And I like that
about you.

White relatives
I like your roads
of course you make
too many of them
and a lot of them
aren't going anywhere
but you make them really well
nevertheless
as if you know where they go and how they'll do
And I like that
about you.

Red relatives
you never start
anything
on time
Time itself
in your thought
not being about
timeliness
so much
as about
time*less*ness.
Powwows could
take forever
and probably do
in your view
and you could care
less.
And I like that
about you.

What can I give you to help you see the soul of our brother or sister stolen from us by too much childhood abuse, too much adulation, too much loneliness, too much money? Too little self reflected in the faces around the home?

The day will come again, as it has already, so many times, when you will see a "successful" person you love who has completely erased the very essence you thought so precious. This will send you into the depths of grief and loss. It is a tragedy that deeply wounds our common psyche. And yet, we must constantly struggle to understand, to be compassionate, to see how we ourselves may have contributed to our own abandonment. We must do this even as we mourn.

I give you:

NATURAL STAR
(*Which I wrote for our little brother, Michael*)

I am in mourning
for your face
The one I used to love
to see leaping, glowing
upon the stage
The mike
eager . . .
Thrusting in your fist.

I am in mourning
for your face
the shining eyes
the happy teeth
the look that said
I *am* the world
and aren't you
glad
Not to mention

deeply
in luck.

I am in mourning
for the sweet brown innocence
of your skin
your perfect nose
the shy smile
that lit you
like a light.

I am in mourning
for a face
the Universe
in its goodness
makes but once
each
thousand years
and smiles
and sends it out
to spread great joy
itself well pleased.

I am in mourning
for your beloved face
so thoroughly and
undeservedly released.

Oh, my pretty little
brother. Genius. Child.
Sing to us. Dance.
Rest in peace.

And what can I give you to help you remember the necessity of
forgiving? On that day when a great wrong has been done to you,
and for which forgiveness seems impossible?

I give you:

GOOD NIGHT, WILLIE LEE,
I'LL SEE YOU IN THE MORNING
(Thereby bringing the spirits of my parents,
Willie Lee and Minnie Tallulah Walker,
into the ceremony of your special day)

Looking down into my father's
dead face
for the last time
my mother said without
tears, without smiles
without regrets
but with *civility*
"Good night, Willie Lee, I'll see you
in the morning."
And it was then I knew that the healing
of all our wounds
is forgiveness
that permits a promise
of our return
at the end.

What can I give you, as women, to remind you of our Goddess-given autonomy, on that day when you realize you are trapped in a situation with another that permits you no more room to grow than a potted geranium on a windowsill?

I give you:

A WOMAN IS NOT
A POTTED PLANT

A woman is not
a potted plant

her roots bound
to the confines
of her house

a woman is not
a potted plant
her leaves trimmed
to the contours
of her sex

a woman is not
a potted plant
her branches
espaliered
against the fences
of her race
her country
her mother
her man

her trained blossom
turning
this way
& that
to follow
the sun
of whoever feeds
and waters
her

a woman
is wilderness
unbounded
holding the future
between each breath
walking the earth
only because
she *is* free
and not creepervine
or tree.

Nor even honeysuckle
or bee.

What can I give you to help you bless the day when you fully
understand that the most basic fact that all patriarchal religions try
to deny and to make people forget is that the Earth is our Mother
and that She must be honored, in order for our days to be long on
this planet?
I give you:

WE HAVE A
BEAUTIFUL MOTHER

We have a beautiful
mother
Her hills
are buffaloes
Her buffaloes
hills.

We have a beautiful
mother
Her oceans
are wombs
Her wombs
oceans.

We have a beautiful
mother
Her teeth
the white stones
at the edge
of the water
the summer grasses
her plentiful
hair.

We have a beautiful
mother
Her green lap
immense
Her brown embrace
eternal
Her blue body
everything
we know.

We are the daughters of Mother Earth: it is in our naturalness and joy in who and what we are that we offer our gratitude, our worship, and our praise.

Beyond this, I give you my word that I shall continue to struggle for and with you, to think of and work for your well-being as women of color, constantly. And to continue to find joy, and freedom, in this. To affirm your strength of character wherever I find myself. Your legendary loyalty and devotion. To honor your beauty and to believe in you without reservation.

I know, from experience, that you are good, and that the world is only made better by your presence.

I love you.

What That Day Was Like for Me

THE MILLION MAN MARCH
OCTOBER 16, 1995

The Flowering of Black Men

In order to watch the Million Man March I had my television repaired. It had been on the blink for six or seven months. Because I allow myself only two hours of television a week, and because I often forget to use those two hours, I hadn't particularly missed it. However, the moment I learned there was to be a march, I knew I wanted to see it. I felt whatever happened would be exciting, instructive, hopeful, and *different*. Television worth watching. Black men have a tradition, after all, of being very interesting.

Lucky for me, a distant neighbor installs dishes (I needed a new one), and though he complained that it was a weekend and that he'd promised to take his son to play soccer, he managed to get everything installed—except for actually digging the trench in which the cable would be laid—within about five hours.

The morning of the march I made my usual bowl of oatmeal and prepared to camp out in front of the television. I don't remember who was speaking when I sat down, but pretty soon there was a young man who reminded me of John Lewis (years ago, of SNCC),* who was exhorting his brothers to "go home" and take on the ills of violence and cocaine. It was a refrain that took me back to the March on Washington of 1963. At that march I sat in a tree listening to Martin Luther King, Jr., asking us to return to the South. I thought then, as I do now, that to ask anyone to go home and work on the problems there is the most revolutionary advice that can be given. Hearing King's words, I packed up and went back to the South, from which I'd fled, like my brothers and sisters before me, and I remained there, writing books, teaching, and doing Movement-related work, for seven years. It was an invaluable time. But one I'm not sure I would have had the courage to give myself if Martin had not spoken so emphatically in favor of it.

Oatmeal finished, still cozy in my jammies, I realized I wanted to hear what every speaker had to say, even if it took the entire day. Which of course it did.

What stands out? The children, most of all. The articulate, poised, and impassioned young boy and the brave, thoughtful, and serious young girl who asked fervently to be *seen* as children, protected, respected, and affirmed by black men. Queen Mother Moore, too old and weary by now even to talk, but still reminding us that, for our suffering and the stolen centuries of our lives, we deserve reparations. Rosa Parks. Jesse Jackson, a major teacher for this period. Clear, courageous, brilliant in his ability to use words to illuminate rather than obfuscate. Making connections. Naming names. Radiating a compassionate wrathfulness. Then, disappearing. Which was its own magic. Louis Farrakhan. Who would have thought he'd try to teach us American history using numerology? I was intrigued. Who even suspected that his mother was West Indian, and that he could not only honor her by recalling her wry humor but share her spirit with us by uttering her Jamaican folk speech? This was the man nobody wanted black leaders to talk to? It seemed bizarre.

---

* The Student Nonviolent Coordinating Committee, a student civil rights organization of the 1960s.

I can't imagine becoming Muslim. Because it is a religion whose male Semitic God demands submission and whose spread, historically, has been primarily through conquest, I consider it unsafe. Anyone who is thinking about converting to Islam should first investigate its traditional application in the Middle East and Africa, and its negative impact on women and children in particular, and also on the environment. They should also read the work of Taslima Nasrin, recently threatened with death in Bangladesh for suggesting changes in Islamic law, and *Why I Am Not a Muslim* by Ibn Warraq.

However, I did not think Farrakhan was proselytizing. I thought he spoke as a black man with a following, and therefore some independence and power, and that the urge to do *something* in these grim and perilous times in which we risk being re-enslaved—by drugs, television, violence, and the seductive traffic on the super-information highway along which most of us will have only a footpath—propelled him. If he is homophobic, as many of my friends believe, this is a great pity, and I assume he was asking forgiveness for that, knowing how black-male-phobic society can be, and how wretched that feels. If he is anti-Semitic (and I thought his son quite beautiful denouncing this charge), he definitely needed to be forgiven, in front of the whole world, and that is what I felt he was asking for. I was moved by him, and underneath all the trappings of Islam, which I personally find frightening, I glimpsed a man of humor, a persuasive teacher, and someone unafraid to speak truth to power, a virtue that makes it easier to be patient as he struggles to subdue his flaws. His speech was a bit long, but I think this was a result of his having always been respectfully listened to by his Muslim congregation. As was clear from the presence of young women in the march, who had been asked to stay home, and of gay men, too, in the larger world, outside the Muslim community, it is only the part of his message that embraces us all that is likely to be heard.

In any event, as someone who has been thrown out of "the black community" several times in my life, and someone who blesses my flaws for all I've learned from them, I found it heart-warming to see Jesse, Ben (Chavis), and Louis assert their right to stand together on issues so large that every one of us will have to strain to keep the race's raggedy boat afloat. I did not feel left out at all. I think it is absolutely necessary that black men regroup as black men; until they can talk to each other, cry with each other, hug and kiss each other, they will never know how to do those things with me. I know whole black men can exist, and I want to see and enjoy them.

I loved the flags! Each one a thrilling testament to our deep feeling of being people of many different nations, capable of coming together for the common good. The beauty of the men themselves was striking. This is the beauty of soul-searching, of spiritual seeking, and, yes, also of recognizing you are lost. It is the beauty all human beings have when they give up the act and settle down to work on the amazing and problematic stuff of life.

After the march ended, and while I was still thinking of the powerful pledge to change lives, directions, communities, that Farrakhan led a million (or two million) black men through, I knew I needed to take a walk, to put my feet on the earth, to see late-flowering shrubs, and to stand among tall trees. I have known black men in my life who are flexible like the grass and sheltering like the trees. But many black men have themselves forgotten they can be this way. It is their own nature that they miss. And they have tried to find it again in drugs, sex, information overload, oppression of women and children, and violence. As I see it, black men have a deep desire to relearn their own loveliness, as Galway Kinnell expresses it in these lines:

> for everything flowers, from within, of self-blessing;
> though sometimes it is necessary
> to reteach a thing its loveliness,
> to put a hand on the brow
> of the flower,
> and retell it in words and in touch,

it is lovely
until it flowers again from within, of self-blessing*

Standing near my house, in a forest that was once ravaged by poorly paid loggers intent on making a profit for rich thieves who do not respect the planet, and finding it still, in its ravaged, struggling-to-recover state, miraculous, I send a prayer to my brothers: that you continue to open to each other and to bless yourselves. Continue to let go of fear. Continue to insist on truth and trust. Our time is short on this earth, but that it can be rich and joyous in spite of oppression, white madness, and black confusion is undeniable. Be each other's "hand on the brow." Don't miss your time.

---

* I first encountered this poem in Sharon Salzberg's wonderful book *Lovingkindness: The Revolutionary Art of Happiness.* The lines are from "St. Francis and the Sow," by Galway Kinnell.

PART FOUR

Turquoise and Coral

*Alice Walker and Robert Allen at Jung's retreat in Bollingen, Switzerland.
Spring, 1987. The photo was taken by our taxi driver, using Robert's camera.*

Turquoise and Coral

THE WRITING OF
THE TEMPLE OF MY FAMILIAR

Painting My Own Door

One day in Mendocino in 1983 I was invited to the home of a casual acquaintance who knew of my interest in Indian art. For sale, spread across her yard, were many items from Guatemala: jewelry, fabrics, clothing, beaded gourds, musical instruments. They were being sold by a Guatemalan man and his North American wife, who said that the money they earned would go to the people from whom they had received the goods: Indians who had been chased from their homes and villages by a Spanish-speaking army led by non-Indians.

There were many old and rare pieces of clothing which looked as if they'd just come off someone's back. I bought one of these, a lovely, well-used shawl of many colors, and an old piece of red-and-blue handwoven cotton, very faded and with a number of holes. This cloth, the North American woman assured me, was practically extinct in Guatemala and was not being made anymore. I liked its colors, its softness. What had it been in its Guatemalan life, I wondered. A tablecloth? A bedspread? For it was large, I saw as I unfolded it beneath the trees prior to purchase. There were curious seams running through it and, along one side, a hem. It had a quality I particularly like—in people as well as in fabric—suppleness and strength.

It was months later, after I had earned enough money to build an indoor toilet onto my studio, that I noticed there were words (actually one word, printed over and over) written on the cloth. I was sitting in the shade on the front deck, making a pair of curtains for the new bathroom (for I had decided to splurge and have a bathtub as well). I held the cloth up to the sun and tried to read it, only to find that the word was in Spanish. Well, my daughter, Rebecca, studied Spanish in school and was practically fluent; I called her immediately and spelled the word for her. It meant "Remember."

Well, yes, I thought, but what am I to remember?

I completed the curtains, hung them at the windows, stroked them often as I passed by, and now the word "*Recuerda*" (which I now saw was only the first half of a much longer word, which Rebecca and I loosely translated as "You all remember!") stood out with all the clarity and impact of a stop sign. I was to remember; I knew that much; and part of what I had to remember, I soon realized, was the condition and fate of the people, women, surely, who had made the cloth.

For years my partner, Robert, and I had planned to study Spanish. Rebecca supported and encouraged us. In the fall of 1986, just at the start of the rainy season, we began classes, tutored by Rebecca's own high school Spanish teacher, Joanna. Each Tuesday morning promptly at ten o'clock she arrived, and we sat around my dining-room table as Robert and I made a valiant attempt to learn Spanish. This continued for five months. I was remarkably slow to learn. Robert, who once spent a summer constructing housing on the outskirts of Havana, was much quicker. I found Spanish as difficult to learn and to speak as it was beautiful to hear—and not at all "easy," as my sister students at Spelman College used to tell me it was when I moaned and groaned over the French I had then chosen to study, and have since forgotten.

However, the Spanish-speaking characters in *The Temple of My Familiar* didn't wait for me to attain proficiency in their tongue. Lucky for me. Almost immediately, after only the second or third lesson—at a time when I barely grasped Joanna's cheery greeting each Tuesday morning of *"¡Hola! ¿Como está?"*—they began speaking, as if I understood every word. Which I did, because though I realized they were speaking in Spanish, I was now able to hear it in English! Usually, now, by the time Joanna arrived at ten, I would have been writing the story involving my Spanish-speaking characters since about seven. I would leap out of bed minutes before her knock and hasten into my clothes and down the stairs to dutifully perform, with Roberto, the day's *dialogo*. I felt at times exasperated that when I opened my mouth, the silvery Spanish sounds coiled just beneath my tongue that I had been immersed in for three hours failed to roll out. Joanna, witnessing my look of surprised perplexity, would often laugh.

At the same time that I was learning Spanish—in order to be able to more accurately "remember" the women of the cloth—I began to dream about, to think about, and to desire to see around me the colors turquoise and coral.* I developed such a fixation on these colors, which I called my "spiritual colors," and I talked so much about needing them—though it was unclear to me in just what way I needed them—that on my fortieth birthday, as we sat down to a surprise dinner for me in our rented house in Ubud, Bali, Rebecca and Robert presented me with a very old, lovely East Indian necklace made of turquoise and coral. It was beautiful. I loved it. I put it on. But I needed something more.

Back in the States I bought coral-colored bedsheets, a coral-and-turquoise lampshade. A coral dress. Turquoise boots. But none of these things helped. I still yearned for these two colors, but not necessarily, I soon realized, to decorate my house with or to wear.

---

* The "coral" I had in mind was not bright red but rather a faded terra-cotta. I thought of it as coral because of the many pieces of coral I'd collected over the years that were that color.

I felt apprehensive too. Sometimes, when I thought about the persistence of these colors in my psyche, my need for them seemed irrational, and made me think of the local women when I was growing up, who developed, usually while pregnant, a passion for starch or white clay, which they sucked on by the hour.

One day I overcame my apprehension enough to buy several gallons of turquoise and coral paint. The woman working on the bathroom painted the bathtub turquoise but balked at painting the walls coral. Too hot, she said. And I was cowed again. However, months later, I went out to the shed and pulled out the paint I had bought. The turquoise was too dark, I found, and the coral too orange. I sat down and began to mix these colors with others—the orange coral I mixed with brown, and the dark turquoise I mixed with white, until I reached the colors I'd held so long in my mind. I then began to paint my bed turquoise and the ceiling above my bed coral. I began to paint my front door.

I felt immediately that this was the right thing to do, and went ahead and painted the bed and the ceiling in a matter of hours, giving myself such a painful case of tendonitis in shoulder and wrist that the door was left half done—for nearly a year. Painting my bed and ceiling in turquoise and coral, however, unlocked the central dream of *The Temple of My Familiar,* the dream about our collusion with the forces that suppress and colonize our spirituality. I saw that our essential "familiar" is our own natural, untamed, "wild" spirit and that its temple is the cosmos, that is, freedom. This dream came complete with temple, familiar, Lissie and Suwelo, and the understanding that I was writing a "romance" (that is to say, a wisdom tale, memory, adventure) that was less about the relationships of human beings to each other than about the relationship of humans (women, in particular) to animals, who, in the outer world, symbolize woman's inner spirit.

This insight was confirmed by the fact that animals—whether I was in the country or the city—were suddenly everywhere in my life. A "watch cat" appeared on my stoop in the city and remained there until the novel was done; various other creatures (birds, deer, snakes, etc.) were constant visitors in the country. The presence of these numerous animals seemed so odd to me, but in an entirely lovely way, that I wrote an essay about the experience, called "The Universe Responds." It seemed to me that the animals I now saw wherever I looked—much like the Spanish-speaking characters who showed up talking at the moment I started to learn Spanish— had decided to wait until it was clear whether I had eyes to see, and then had decided to let themselves be seen.

There is a third "leg" on which the pot of this novel rests. It was something that occurred a few months after I'd finished *The Color Purple* and was missing the characters in that book dreadfully. Are there to be no more such fascinating folks in my life? I inwardly mumbled. As I thought about this one day on my way to put a bundle of trash into the outdoor garbage can, I suddenly flashed on an old man in a nursing home and a younger, middle-aged man sitting beside his bed. There was an intensity between them that stopped me in my tracks, and a vividness to the image that made it memorable. I found I was able to recall it, and puzzle over it, clearly and frequently, over the next several years. It was not until I reached the last chapter of *The Temple of My Familiar,* however, that I understood that the old man was Hal and the younger man Suwelo, and that Hal had been instructing Suwelo about how to live—with women, with children, with other men, with animals, with white people. *¡Con todos!*

Throughout the writing of *Temple* I relied on the guidance provided by the synchronicity I experienced between my dreams, insights, and intuitions and events that corroborated or resonated with them in the world. For example, six months or so after I'd written the chapters about the Latin American refugees, Zedé and Carlotta, I met three refugees—a mother and her two young daughters—from El Salvador. I met them at a political demonstration, and for nearly two months they lived in my house with me. We are friends today and I love them all for who they are, but on first meeting, I have to admit, they were the mother and daughter, Zedé and Carlotta, I had created in the opening chapters of my novel, and I responded to them with the instant recognition of someone who already understood something of their lives. It was as if, having written about a refugee family—Zedé and Carlotta—I could now *see* Marcia and her daughters, Maria and Daniela,[*] and they were not, even from the first moment, strangers to me.

I cannot recount or even remember all the times I said to Rebecca or Robert, "Wait till you read my novel!" as some confirmation or other from the Universe appeared. Near the end of writing it, I felt as if I were walking in a circle of magic, and this made me indescribably happy. But nothing could have prepared me for the "magic" that occurred on the very last day of writing. I had just completed the paragraph in which Suwelo contemplates the painting of Lissie as Lion, and was hurrying up the hill to my studio to type it up on my Mac Plus, when I noticed what appeared to be a tan plastic dry cleaner's bag—without my glasses this was a blur—lying some distance out in the field. A neatnik to my soul—I will pick up trash anywhere—I moved quickly to remove this unsightly object, wondering all the while how it came to be there. But then, when I was a few steps away, I saw that it wasn't a discarded dry cleaner's bag but a large, tawny cat, a miniature "lion," lying at ease, calmly looking back at me. I'd never seen it before; I haven't seen it since. I began to smile and fairly skipped along to my studio.

I felt that this "omen" was Lissie's sign of approval for the ending I'd just written, and also a sign from the animals that in *The Temple of My Familiar* I had kept to our collective vision of reality. And that we were united in our sense of peace at the outcome.

And, finally, after the novel was finished in manuscript, I discovered I was ready to complete the painting of my front door, which I had started nearly a year earlier when I painted my ceiling and my bed. Rolling up my sleeves one morning, paintbrush in hand—and only just then realizing I'd written a book in which many of the characters are painters!—I began.

[*] Not their real names.

My door is coral and turquoise, trimmed in dark lavender blue. There is a sun on it and a moon, and the lower turquoise panels look like ocean and the upper ones look like sky. There are two birds flying at the very top. There are snakes left and right.

This is the door to my dwelling. It says: This is the person who lives in this house now.

I look at it, and it is very satisfying to me, though my snakes are awkwardly drawn and my birds are smudged.

Maybe I am mistaken, I think, looking at it, in believing that it was painting with my "spiritual colors," turquoise and coral, that allowed me to write my novel. Perhaps it was writing my novel that permitted me, at last, to paint and therefore to recognize my own door.

POSTSCRIPT: On February 2, 1989, I received the bound reader's copy of *The Temple of My Familiar,* with its dreadlocked lion in one red slipper on the cover.

That night, a chunky raccoon appeared at my back door and looked in on a friend and me as we were finishing supper. We dropped to hands and knees and "talked" to it through the glass, hardly believing what we saw. This was, after all, the back door of my house in the city, which is surrounded not by forest but by other houses and fenced-in backyards, and is in the heart of San Francisco.

Looking for Jung

WRITING POSSESSING THE SECRET OF JOY

In the spring of 1990 my Dutch publisher invited me to Amsterdam. My novel *The Temple of My Familiar* had recently appeared in Holland and I agreed to do a number of signings and readings. A strong motive for going to Amsterdam, which I was delighted to find I liked, was its proximity to Switzerland. One day near the end of our stay in Amsterdam my companion, Robert Allen, and I flew to Zurich and dropped by the C. G. Jung Institute for directions on how to get to Jung's summer retreat at Bollingen, on the shores of Lake Zurich.

We traveled light, as we often do, absorbed in the journey, open to what we always expect will be interesting events. On this trip, as on so many others, we were not disappointed. Though at first no one we encountered at the institute seemed to know a thing about the whereabouts of Bollingen and seemed somewhat surprised we'd want to know how to get there—two middle-aged, dread-locked hippies from the United States, reggae singers, for all they knew—we were not daunted, but decided to wander about the garden to see what flowers the institute had. As we walked away, however, we were flagged by a small blond woman who introduced herself as Susan, and who exclaimed, when I told her my name, that she and her study group had finished reading *The Temple of My Familiar* just the week before. She stared in disbelief that I should be standing there, in Zurich, on the grounds of the Jung Institute. Robert and I laughed at her surprise. After all, we said, as a student of Jung, she should know a thing or two about synchronicity!

Susan was an American who'd been living in Switzerland and studying at the institute for a couple of years. We told her that we wanted to visit Jung's tower-house in Bollingen and that we had only one day to do it in; we had a return flight to Amsterdam the same day. She looked skeptical but immediately told us which train to catch; then, thinking of how fast we'd have to move to get there and back, she decided to come with us and put us on the train herself.

We dashed to the train station, Susan bought our tickets, and within minutes we were on our way, her serious reservations about whether we'd get anywhere near Jung's house ringing in our ears. She had said no one lived there; that the place was behind a high wire fence and a gate that was kept padlocked. Jung's son or grandson sometimes used it, she thought, but she herself had gone to Bollingen on several occasions and had not been able to get in. It was clear she didn't think we'd have much luck getting inside either; it was just as clear she was delighted to help us try.

Since we were on the train, going in the right direction, Robert and I happily settled down to enjoy the ride. Once, we had to change trains, unexpectedly, and encountered a group of Peruvian Indians playing flutes under a bridge. We were so glad to see them, gentle people of color from our own continent, that we might have stayed to listen all afternoon and missed the train to Bollingen. But we made it, and in due course found ourselves somewhere beyond our destination, with the train's conductor telling us we'd have to get off someplace we'd never heard of and walk back.

The town we came to was tiny, but every little restaurant in it seemed to be preparing lunch. We realized we were hungry. After a leisurely meal we sat in the town square admiring the mountains, massive foothills of the Alps, and the lake, its blue edge rimmed by rustling cattails and whispering willows. Pretty soon a new gold-colored Mercedes arrived. A native—florid, flaxen, fifty—leaned from it and said he was the taxi. Would we like to go somewhere? We said we'd like to go to Bollingen. He said, "Get in." We did. Where in Bollingen would we like to go? "Jung's place," we said. He thought he knew where that was, he said. Off we went.

Fifteen minutes later we were passing a large barn in a rolling landscape studded with cows. On a dirt road that runs parallel to the lake we met a tall, elderly, white-haired man who appeared out of nowhere and caused me to do a double take. Our driver waved at him, the elderly man hoisted his pipe in response, and we sped on down the road. Robert and I held hands tightly, not knowing what to expect. We remembered Susan's warning that the high wire gate was always locked. That on not one of her journeys over a two-year period had she been able to get inside.

Well, there ahead of us was the gate. It was standing wide open. The driver stopped and we all got out of the car.

Since he'd brought us where we wanted to go, we tried to pay him and send him on his way, asking him to return for us in a bit. But no. He asked us, "Don't you want to go inside the gate?" "More than anything," I said. But even after coming so far, I couldn't bring myself to trespass. I stood craning my neck and standing on tiptoe, trying to get a glimpse of something, anything, through the trees.

"No, no," our guide said, dismissing my efforts. And off he went through the gate and down to the house. In a few minutes we heard him knocking on a door. Voices. Soon we saw him striding back, smiling and beckoning us forward.

Suddenly, there it was. The lake, the thick stone walls of the tower. The door to the courtyard. Once more I hesitated. Perhaps the people inside had said yes to the guide. Perhaps they'd say no to us. I felt we should give them a second chance. I asked the guide to knock again. A voice said, "Come in." Robert and I stood in the doorway long enough to be denied admittance, but there was no sign of that. Four young people, two men and two women, lazed about in the small yard by the lake, basking like geckos in the warm sun. We asked if we might look around. They said sure. And look around we did. Inside and outside the tower. In the loggia, Robert photographed me sitting in the sun in the doorway of the main house, and again with my fingers just grazing Jung's hand-carved alchemical stone,* the stone that represents both transformation and transcendence. The guide/taxi driver photographed both of us. I stood transfixed before the symmetry of Jung's woodpile.

---

* This image would form the basis for the painting on the cover of *Possessing the Secret of Joy.*

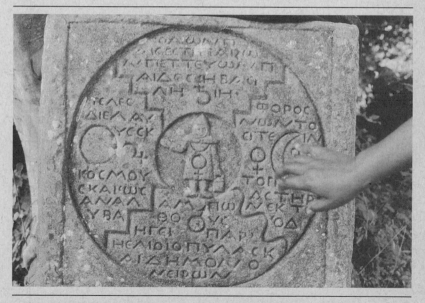

Alice touching Jung's alchemical stone, prior to writing Possessing the Secret of Joy, *a novel about the physical, and especially the psychological, devastation caused by female genital mutilation. Spring, 1987.*

PHOTO BY ROBERT ALLEN

We stayed for half an hour, admiring more carved stones, stone towers, and lakeside view. Then, after thanking the young people, who seemed somewhat dazed by the sun, we were whisked to the Bollingen train station and sent on our way to Zurich. We were back in Amsterdam the same night.

We fell asleep in our quiet hotel room overlooking a canal, exhausted but content. I felt especially fulfilled; I knew this was the last journey I had to make before beginning to write *Possessing the Secret of Joy,* a story whose subject frankly frightened me. An unpopular story. Even a taboo one. An ancient story. A modern story. A story in which I would call on Jung's spirit to help me confront one of the most physically and psychologically destructive practices of our time (and of thousands of years before our time), a practice that undermines the collective health and wholeness of great numbers of people in Africa, the Middle East, and the Far East and is rapidly finding a toehold in the Western world: the genital mutilation of women and girls.

Frida, the Perfect Familiar

Poking a Hole Through

Five years ago I decided I was ready to share my life with a cat. I had had cats before, but things had gone wrong. When I was seven, we moved away from the house where my cat and I lived. She could not be found as my family packed, and so she was left behind. I missed her terribly, and hardened my heart against future attachments to creatures who might disappear. Since any creature one loves is likely to disappear, this was a major disservice to my heart. It was closed down, made smaller. The next cat I had was given to me and my daughter by a friendly publicist at my publishing company. Her name was Willis and my friend Hilda had rescued her from the Willis Avenue Bridge in New York City. As one would expect, given the heavy traffic on the bridge and the horrendous noise of its rattles and creaks, Willis was thoroughly traumatized. No matter. She was a living gift and therefore not returnable. It is fair to say that for the duration of our time with Willis we suffered right along with her. Feeding her, attempting to pet her, providing a place for her to sleep, murmuring sweet cajolings and endearments while she looked over her shoulder in terror, as if she expected at any moment to be run over.

She would also cry. After several years our relationship became unendurable. One day as I was working and she was loudly crying, I picked her up, took her outside the building I was living in, in San Francisco, and left her. When my partner came home that evening, there she was, sitting in the flowerbed, still crying, still haunted. I looked very much a villain. I didn't care. Noting this, my partner offered to take Willis to live with his sister, a saintly woman who loved animals, especially wounded ones, and who had as well the saintly name Teresa. This was good news to me. Willis retired to the Sierra foothills, where Teresa lived, and according to my partner, who visited his sister often, in the utter peace of spacious woodlands and sunny skies Willis mellowed into a rather laid-back country cat.

Prior to this, while I still lived in New York, I had been given another cat. My husband and I had divorced; we shared custody of our daughter, and she took Willis with her when she stayed with him for a while. A well-meaning friend, seeing me catless, lonely, and crazed with the unexpected grief that only divorce can leave you, thought she had the answer to my needs. I named this cat Tuscaloosa, which means "Black Warrior" in Choctaw. As is clear from his name, I felt extremely vulnerable, suddenly all alone in the big city, and very much in need of protection. I have only good memories of him. We lived in a tiny three-room, second-story flat in Park Slope, Brooklyn; our landlords were civil and understanding gay white men who sometimes let Tuscaloosa play in their garden. Often, as I worked at my desk, which overlooked the street, Tuscaloosa sat at my feet. More often I wrote propped-up in bed; he snoozed, placid and warm, by my knees. Alas, after a year or so, I knew it was time to leave that apartment, leave Brooklyn, leave New York and the East Coast. I knew I would move to San Francisco, but not where I would live. I also knew, because my daughter told me, that Willis would soon be back in my life. Fortunately, Tuscaloosa had made friends with Chad, the little boy who lived upstairs, whose father was never around, and after discussing it with his mother, I decided to leave Tuscaloosa with him.

For many years after the departures of Willis and Tuscaloosa I felt delightfully cat free. I had learned to meditate while still in Brooklyn; it was the only thing, other than time, that helped me recenter after my divorce. But I had also learned that any still, calmly breathing, warm object with a lap immediately attracts the leap of a cat. I could not shut Tuscaloosa away in another part of the flat. During my twenty minutes, morning and evening, of meditation, he'd scratch and complain until, exasperated, I opened the door. Nor could I ask my landlords to let him play in their garden every day. So now, as I sat in my new study in San Francisco, on a worn but sturdy couch I got from a salvage warehouse, and blissfully meditated without fear of intrusion or distraction, I was deeply conscious of being at peace. A cat, I thought, would ruin it.

Years went by.

Shortly after arriving in San Francisco I had been fortunate, with the help of my partner, to find a place in the country in which to dream, meditate, and write. A year or so after being there I reconnected with the world of animals and spirits—in trees, old abandoned orchards, undisturbed riverbanks—I had known and loved as a child. I became aware that there is a very thin membrane, human-adult-made, that separates us from this seemingly vanished world, where plants and animals still speak a language we humans understand, and I began to write about the exhilarating experience of regaining my childhood empathy.

I discovered that not only is there an adult-made membrane separating us from animals, rocks, rivers and trees, ocean and sky, there is one separating us from our remote ancestors, who are actually so near that they are us. I began to write *The Temple of My Familiar,* a book that immediately became my home, just as the land I lived on became the home of more and more animals, who, I sometimes joked with my partner, had somehow gotten word that this was going to be a breakthrough book. They seemed to know I had managed to poke a hole through the membrane that separated me from them, and they roamed the land: slithering, crawling, stalking, flying, in a steady, amazing wave. I've written elsewhere of the captive horse looking for refuge that suddenly appeared, the flocks of wild turkeys, the feral pigs. The eagles, the snakes, and the hawks. It really did seem as if word had gone out: There's harmlessness over at Alice's! I was in heaven and I knew it; I realized that this experience and others like it are "the gold and diamonds and rubies" of life on radiant earth. On the day I finished the book, and while I still lived in it as an ancestor who was very tight with a lion, and as an even earlier ancestor who *was* a lion, I saw a miniature "lion" lying in the grass as I walked up the hill to my studio. I knew it was time to invite into my life another cat.

My partner was skeptical, reminding me of my poor track record. That I was often on the road; that I can abide only a certain amount of responsibility or noise. The yearning persisted. I was only too aware of my limitations, and hesitated a year or more. I asked my daughter what she thought: Was I mature enough to have this anticipated companion in my life? She thought yes. And so the two of us began making the rounds of shelters, looking at cats. Most had been abandoned, most were starved. Most were freaked-out but exhibited some degree of calm in whatever shelter they were in, where they were fed and kept dry and warm, and where, at the shelter we especially liked, there were young women and men who periodically opened the cages and brought the cats out for brushing, claw clipping, or a cuddle. It was here that we found Frida, a two-year-old long-haired calico with big yellow eyes and one orange leg. She was so bored with shelter life that on each of our visits she was sound asleep. Still, even in sleep, she had presence. We woke her up and took her home.

Alas, like Willis, Frida was afraid of everything, even of caresses. She jumped at the slightest noise. For months she ran and hid whenever anyone, including me, came into the house. Brushing her was difficult because she could not abide being firmly held. Her long hair became shaggy and full of burrs. The guests who tried to pet her were scurried from; to show her dislike of them, she pooped on their bed. Much of her day was spent on the top shelf of a remote closet, sleeping.

I named her Frida, after Frida Kahlo. I could only hope she'd one day exhibit some of Kahlo's character. That despite her horrendous kittenhood she would, like Kahlo, develop into a being of courage, passion, and poise.

When Frida wasn't sleeping, I discovered the Universe had played a very serious joke on me. Ever since I was a child I have needed the peace and quiet of morning. Everyone in my life, since I became an adult, has respected this. No one calls me, no one dares intrude for any reason, before noon. Frida made herself the exception. She was an exceedingly garrulous cat. She set out every morning to tell me the latest installment of her sad, heartrending tale, six or seven lives long, and she chatted steadily for an hour or so. When I was thoroughly rattled, she stopped, went upstairs, and took a nap.

This was our entirely inauspicious beginning.

Being an activist means I travel, a lot. Sometimes to other cities and countries, but also between my city and country homes. I took to carrying Frida, when I could catch her, with me. I have memories of careening around mountain curves with Frida, terrified, stuck to my neck. I was unable to endure the piteous cries she emitted when I secured her in a cage. When not stuck to my neck or in my hair, she sought safety underneath the brake pedal. I eventually resolved to leave her in the country—she hid when she saw me packing to return to the city. I did this reluctantly, acknowledging defeat. I asked M, the caretaker, to make sure she had water, food, and surrogate affection.

Time passed. Sometimes I would be away for a month or more. When I returned, Frida would have taken up at a neighbor's house. After a few days, she'd return. Distant and cool. I would struggle to renew our bond, beating myself up in my guilt. By the time we were back to the point of Frida's warily permitting a tentative stroke, I'd be off again. Sometimes when I came home she'd be hiding in the oak tree by the drive, or in the bay tree off the deck. If I brought anyone with me, she'd sit and watch us but never deign to appear. Sometimes when I returned she'd simply cry. And cry and cry. It was a sound that went straight to my heart.

And yet, this was my life. I thought perhaps Frida would one day simply get tired of it and leave me. She is very beautiful, very smart; I didn't think it impossible that she would, on her own, find a more suitable home. There were also times, after cleaning poop off the rug or the guest bed, that I wanted to help her relocate.

More time passed. One day I noticed that Frida understood English. If I said, "I don't want you to lie on my chest because there's a book there at the moment that I'm reading," and if I patted the spot by my thigh that was okay, she immediately settled there. If she knocked at the window and I said, "Just a minute," she'd wait before coming to the door. I noticed that instead of dodging my caress, she sought it. On our walks, if I sat down to enjoy a view, she did too. Around that same time I stopped criticizing myself constantly for not being home all the time, or even most of it. If I was in too bad a mood to stroke or brush her and if, God forbid, I forgot to give her milk, which I always brought and which she expected, I didn't think I was an awful person. I stopped worrying that somewhere there was probably a better companion than I was. We were the companion each of us had found, and I began to see that, in fact, we had a relationship.

Today Frida recognizes the sound of my car, a sluggish black Saab convertible that chugs up the hill to our house, and on whose warm cloth top she likes to sleep. When I approach our gate, after the long drive from the city, I see her huge yellow eyes staring out beneath it. By the time I am out of the car she is at my side, chatting away. She accompanies me into the house, asking for milk, and as soon as I've put my things away, she stretches out on the rug in anticipation of a cuddle and a brush. If I'm not into her yet, she understands, and goes back to her milk or, with a querulous complaint, "Where were you, anyhow? What took you so long?" she claims her favorite spot on the couch—which is everybody else's favorite too.

When she sees me putting on boots and grabbing my walking stick, she leaps up, tail like a bushy flag, and beats me to the door. At first she talks as we walk, but then she falls silent, running alongside me exactly as a dog would. Sometimes she's distracted by field mice, but usually she does her hunting and gathering while I'm in the house; she likes to bring fresh mouse and leave it by the door. The little corpse, its neck chewed through, is, I know, Frida's bouquet. At night she watches me make a fire, plump the sofa pillows, lie down and cover myself with a quilt. She climbs promptly onto my chest and gives my breast a thorough kneading. This always makes me think of Frida's mother and wonder about her fate. As the fire dances we listen to stories: Clarissa Pinkola Estés or Joseph Campbell; or music: Salif Keita, Youssou N'dour, Rachel Bagby, Bonnie Raitt, Tina Turner, or Al Green; Labi Siffre, Digable Planets, or Archie Roach; Phoebe Snow or Deep Forest; Sade. She likes music, except when it's loud. Purring, she stretches her considerable length—she is quite a big cat—and before falling asleep she always reaches up, with calm purpose, to touch my face. "Watch those claws," I always say.

When it is bedtime I pick her up, cuddle her, whisper what a sweet creature she is, how beautiful and wonderful, how lucky I am to have her in my life, and that I will love her always. I take her to her room, with its cat door for her *après*-midnight exitings, and gently place her on her bed. In the morning when I wake up she is already outside, quietly sitting on the railing, eyes closed, meditating.

PART FIVE

The Growth of Understanding

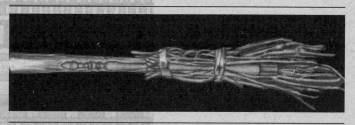

The broom, the pen, and one's body can be used to stir things up.
This is their connection to and kinship with Nature. With the wind,
especially. Which stirs, blows away what is useless and dead, and
cleanses to make new.

PHOTO BY SUE SELLARS, ARTIST AND NEIGHBOR <u>EXTRAORDINAIRE</u>,
SEPTEMBER, 1996.

Giving the Party

Who Do You Think

One thing that never ceases to amaze me, along with the growth of vegetation from the earth and of hair from the head, is the growth of understanding. It isn't something you have to run after with a net, and you don't exactly stumble over it. It just seems to wait inside to be uncovered in leisurely fashion, at the most unexpected moments.

My mother was large when I was a child, her weight averaging around two hundred pounds, and because of her Cherokee and Scotch-Irish ancestry she was paler of skin than many of the mothers in our rural community. She was a maid, though, like some of them, and worked in the homes of white people. Because of this work and her size, and her broad smile—when she smiled, for she also had a frown that could make you sit down—I must have been reminded of her the first time I encountered a likeness of "Aunt Jemima." I would have seen Aunt Jemima first on a box of grits, which my mother cooked in quantity and ladled out lavishly. Later I would see her in films about the antebellum ("before de war")

South, playing a truly described "supporting role" to skinny white stars like Bette Davis, her huge bulk demonstrating what would happen if white women didn't limit their appetites and submit to having their stays pulled tight. I'm sure we laughed, my siblings and I. After all, she was so ridiculous. Her teeth so many and so white, her eyes so wide. Her devotion to her whitefolks so extreme.

Through the years, because of the unspoken connection I felt between Aunt Jemima, "Mammy," and my mother, I've struggled with this image. For generations in the South it was the only image of a black woman that was acceptable. You could be "Aunt" Jemima, sexless and white-loving, or you could be unseen. There were Aunt Jemima dolls that sprawled in shops where black women could not try on dresses. There were ashtrays, cookie jars, lemonade dispensers. Everywhere you looked, that open, beaming, fat black face. Guileless. Without any attempt to fool you. Here I am, the smile said. I will neither reject nor judge you. After all, I am yours.

For many years I did not make the connection that "mammy" was derived from "mammae," that is, breasts. And that when white people had an Aunt Jemima around the house and called her Mammy, it was the same as calling her Tits. Go ask Tits to give you a drink of milk, they were really saying to their children. Go ask Tits for a sip of water or a piece of bread. Tits. It was Tits who had wet-nursed many of these people as infants because their own mothers, not wanting to ruin their stick figures, refused.

One day I flew across country and made a stop at the airport in Dallas. I was coming from San Francisco, where recently a popular cookbook written by a white man had appeared with a giant Aunt Jemima/Mammy on the cover. I never picked it up, though I saw it everywhere. I felt insulted by the image and by a white person's appropriation of it. In the airport I ambled along, looking in all the book and gift shops. In the gift shops there were rows and rows of Aunt Jemima/Mammy dolls. Jet black, grinning cloth faces, huge hoop earrings, the ever-present and colorful bandanna wrapped around her head. Only in New Orleans, on a visit years before, had I seen a greater number and variety. This was at a time, in the Sixties, when black people everywhere were struggling to define their own identity. The reaction of white racists was to stock their stores with images that demonstrated their resistance to this liberating behavior. Sambos, jockeys, Jemimas, Hoodoo queens, abounded. I picked up one of the dolls and looked at it closely. "Did you already buy that?" drawled the clerk. "No," I said, "I never did." I put "Tits" down and ambled on to the cafeteria.

And there she was. A half dozen of her. Some large, some not. Some middle-aged, some quite young. No one of a size or age to compete with Hattie McDaniel, or the hefty sister on the grits box, or my mother. But dressed in long, flouncy antebellum dresses. With large, shiny hoop earrings, and with the obligatory plump and somehow ridiculous bandanna. Texas was hanging on to its version of its past, where there was always a big fat black woman standing next to a big black pot. Well, they were, these real-life Jemimas, standing next to pots; black miniatures of the ones "Tits" and her sisters labored over in the capacious open fireplaces of "before de war." Using large black spoons, the women ladled out beans and soup and gravy and rice. Their faces dignified, reserved, even serene. It occurred to me that the black woman is herself a symbol of nurturing, and that these women, throughout all their incarnations in this country, and for millennia before they arrived here, would have been standing or sitting just so, in whatever tribe or clan, being sure that everyone was fed. In other words, what I was seeing, as if for the first time, was a very ancient image which the modern world, quite without knowing why, had found impossible to do without. As I picked up my tray and started through the line I smiled, for I felt something sweet coming over me. A sureness. A peace. It was, in fact, the belated recognition that I was in the presence of the Goddess, She who nurtures all, and that no matter how disguised, abused, ridiculed, she may be, even white supremacists have been unable to throw her away. And She is with us still. Furthermore, I realized I loved Her.

Some years later, on my way to a winter retreat in Mexico, I pick up a weekly magazine on the plane. There's an article about an exuberantly racist radio talk-show host, all the rage, apparently, in New York City, and one thing he said strikes me as particularly interesting. "The closest I've ever come to going to bed with a black woman," he said (presumably to the snickering laughter of his radio audience), "was to masturbate while thinking of Aunt Jemima." When I go grocery shopping in the local village I am thinking of this, mulling it over, as I fill my bag with *leche, arroz, queso, tortillas,* and half a dozen cans of *jugo de durazno,* which I love. The village is named after the revolutionary Emiliano Zapata, and large men on small burros still meander past; there are always lots of laughing children playing in the dusty street. Everyone is brown and seems healthy, though on first take the village—which has no plumbing or sewage system, no paved streets—looks poor. As I await my turn at the counter I glance about the small *tienda* and notice that above the door, where in many establishments here there is a painting of the Virgen de Guadaloupe, there is instead a black-and-white photograph of Marilyn Monroe. Her lipstick seems to have been spread on with a butter knife, her false eyelashes sweep her cheeks. She is pale as death itself. Sleeping with her, I think, would be like sleeping with a clown. And yet I recognize the relatedness of this image—dead white sex symbol—to that of "Tits" Jemima. Know that one's tits were for nourishment, the other's for play. And that this image of Monroe, of any white woman who resembles her, is the consciously desired object. The consciously desired, by white men especially, image of the goddess. The only problem is that—though her image hangs over the door of this Mexican man's corner market, displacing the brown Virgen de Guadaloupe, which I'm sure used to be there—she is just hanging in midair, made-up, possibly drugged, doing nothing. Certainly she is not near the food. Not near the cooking pots. As goddess (sex goddess, they've named her, these men who've created her in their own image of themselves as women), what would Monroe actually be able to provide? I contemplate her image as I walk out the door. If anything, her dazed and vacant look promises emptiness. Oblivion. Did the men who slept with her—the Kennedys,

Sinatra, and the rest—wake up from her bed needier than before? No doubt. And when she washed off the makeup and rolled up the eyelashes and wasn't even the female clown they went to bed with, what then?

If Jemima is Tits, I think, driving home, avoiding the self-possessed white cows who wander across the road, then Monroe is Cunt. And she is Cunt for a very good reason. Cunts give birth. Tits, strictly speaking—and this separation of function between the black woman and the white has been done strictly—do not. If you're a white man, you can fantasize having sex with Monroe and even fantasize a child as the result. Tits Jemima, though, that's another thing. She might be your food supply from birth, but the white-supremacist society has done everything in its power to make her unacceptable as the mother of your child. She cannot ever be perceived as a goddess. Certainly not. Of any kind.

And yet. There she is, in the Dallas, Texas, airport. Her big tits right next to the big black pot; a potent symbol, the big black pot, in itself. For isn't the black pot of a black woman's womb the vessel from which white men secretly fear they came, just as the big black hole in the cosmos is the black pot into which they fear they will disappear? Who else worries about such things? In any case, there she is. She's making almost nothing at this shitty job, and her children are probably at home alone in a cold house, being baby-sat by television, watching shows in which the white mother's child wants for nothing. But Tits Jemima's stirring something warm and it smells good. And when you come forward in your hunger, you don't even have to ask. She just says, "Chile, you looks hongry. Have some of this soup." What are you going to do?

At night I sit up in bed, a chilled glass of *jugo de durazno* in hand, and I listen to a tape by Marion Woodman. She is a well-known Canadian psychoanalyst with a not-very-soothing voice. Just before I give up on the tape she says a startling thing. She mentions that in the dreams of her analysands, and in those of more and more people in the world, a surprising and specific figure is appearing. Guess who? It is the figure, Woodman says, of a large black or "chocolate" woman. Woodman calls her the Black Madonna.

I listen, enchanted. Realizing the world is, at long last, turning. And from the inside out. Tits Jemima, I think. There in the unconscious, where she's always been, most internal and external doors slammed against her.

I drain my glass of peach juice, which connects me to the land of Jemimas, my beautiful mother, and my Georgia home, and permit myself a thought about the private sexual behavior of the racist radio talk-show host. There he is, chalk-white fingers wrapped around his fat, putty-colored weenie. He is pumping away, staring deeply (he likes to think) into the vacant, vaguely come-hither eyes of Marilyn Monroe, who gazes druggedly down from a photograph on his bedroom wall. In her grave she is a skeleton, but he doesn't think of that. He pumps and he pumps, closing his eyes, visualizing those eyes, those cheeks, those lips under their crust of lipstick, those milky breasts which have never held milk. Marilyn, Madonna, he croons, rotating his awkward hips. Where shall he stick it? he is wondering, when all of a sudden he realizes Marilyn—her mouth, her tits, her cunt, and her ass—has completely disappeared. A large warm brownness beckons him. He is so offended that he will not at first acknowledge it as the body of a woman, or look at her face. When he does look, in the urgency of his orgasm, which he is not quite racist enough to forgo, he sees it is the face and body of one who has always accepted him as he was, fed him, and given him haven between those enormous, mountainlike breasts. He tries to pull back, to find Marilyn or Madonna or some other acceptable image, but can't. Sleeping with Madonna, he thinks, would be like working for the Mafia. You'd have to toe the line. Marilyn would probably be sleeping off her sleeping pills. And besides, didn't she die some years ago? Coming, he remembers black baby-sitters and maids his parents employed when he was a child, and how, against his feeble will, they charmed him. He thinks of Aunt Jemima, and how he will have to make a joke out of this experience for his radio show. He thinks this will prove he is still in control.

Woodman tells one analysand's dream: She is at a large outdoor party and there are many people present, all eating and drinking and making merry. In the middle of the very large lawn there is a cage, and in this cage there is a large black woman. The dreamer goes up to the woman in the cage and says, "What are you doing in there?" The large woman replies, "Who do you think is giving the party?"

Who indeed.

In the airport in Dallas, Texas, a place I associate with the assassination of the only United States president who made me laugh, that is the question that was answered for me. As I sat that day, eating my soup across from the Aunt Jemimas behind the counter, I looked carefully into each one's face. They were tired, yes. I could tell their feet hurt. But I did not see stinginess. I did not see meanness. I did not see cruelty or greed. I knew that left to themselves, they would—any one of them—feed me if I said I was hungry and had no money to pay. Because that's who they were. The ones giving the party. The ones caged in the foolish antebellum dresses and Aunt Jemima bandannas. The ones kept out of sight by being made grotesquely visible. The Goddess who can never be thrown away, for though she is caged, that is only because she is inside us.

POSTSCRIPT: Months after publishing this essay I discovered that Jemima was the name of the eldest of three daughters born to Job after Yahweh repaid his faith by removing all afflictions from him and restoring to him all that he had formerly possessed, and more. The name means "daybreak," "God's blessing," "prosperity."

Treasure

*A statement read upon acceptance of the
California Governor's Award for Literature,
March 25, 1994.*

If We Are to Be Treasures,
Let Us Demand to Be Treasured

A few months ago I was informed I had been chosen
for this award, which would designate me a "treasure" of the State
of California. Because I love California, this appealed to me.
Unfortunately, a few weeks later I learned that a short story and an
essay of mine had been removed from the California State
Achievement Test, which is administered to tenth-graders. My
story was termed anti-religious by a fundamentalist Christian
group called the Coalition for Traditional Values. The essay was
described as anti–meat eating, which would be, presumably, an
insult to the meat-eating tenth-graders of the state, who would be
taking the test.

Of course, if one's work is censored out of the curriculum of the
state's children so easily, and with such flimsy excuses, there is no
point pretending one is a state treasure. I declined the designation.

It was only after hundreds and thousands of people sprang into
action, individually and through various organizations—teachers,
students, writers, journalists, state and national educators, legisla-

tors, the N.A.A.C.P., the National Writers Union, People for the American Way, and the American Civil Liberties Union, to name a few—and publicly denounced the decision of the Department of Education, that my story and essay were returned to the pool of literature that will be used for future tests.

Without this activity, I would not be here. I would consider this ceremony itself meaningless. I accept the designation of "state treasure" in the name of those who fought for my work. And for your right, and our children's right, to enter, with understanding, a larger world. You have very passionately and beautifully affirmed my value to you, and so the term rightly belongs to me. Thank you.

I want each of you to know that just as I now accept the designation "a treasure" of our state, you are each, individually, and all of you, collectively, a treasure to me. And I have something to ask of you.

Even more offensive than anti-religious and anti-meat-eating views to the Christians who sought to suppress my work was the fact that the primary character in my story is a black unwed mother. (They have clearly forgotten Mary and seem never to have heard of the birth of Jesus.) They did not wish to give this young woman any space at all in society, not even in the imagination of our children. And yet, I ask you, what is the point of the rest of us being treasures to each other if any unwed mother, black or otherwise, is denied? She is the most isolated, the most vulnerable, the most scared, and, I believe, the most sacred.

And this is what I ask of you: to the long list of California's endangered treasures—you, me, the wild rivers, the black bear, the spotted owl, and the redwood tree—consciously add the unwed mother. We, as a society, have left her alone too long, with results that are obvious to us all. Indeed, society's treatment of her reflects the abandonment and neglect of that other scorned and unprotected mother of us all: Mother Earth. And see how angry and disgusted She has become with us.

If we are to be treasures, let us demand to be treasured.

And let our awareness of, and tenderness to, the most helpless be our diamonds and our gold. Our last five minutes on Earth are running out. We can spend those minutes in meanness, exclusivity, and self-righteous disparagement of those who are different from us, or we can spend them consciously embracing every glowing soul who wanders within our reach. Those who, without our caring, would find the vibrant, exhilarating path of Life just another sad and forsaken road.

Perhaps the greatest treasure left to us, maybe the only one, is that we can still choose.

Heaven Belongs to You

WARRIOR MARKS
AS A LIBERATION FILM

*Remarks made at the Grand Lake Theater,
Oakland, California, on the screening
of* Warrior Marks, *February 24, 1994.*

You Still Have a Life to Live

The film you are about to see is only one of many efforts we will have to make to change the practice of female genital mutilation. Efforts which will undoubtedly be the work of many generations.

I was talking this afternoon to my friend the director of the film, Pratibha Parmar, who lives in London. She told me that the wife of the man who was our driver while we were filming in Africa had recently been in Britain. And that she was distraught because her husband, whom we had all liked so much, and who was very aware of the dangers and pain involved in female genital mutilation—and who also knew why we had come to Africa to make our film— had nonetheless permitted his own daughters to be mutilated. His excuse: Mutilation is "women's business." The wife is Scottish. The husband Gambian. The children who have been mutilated are by his first wife, a Gambian woman, for whom female genital mutilation is custom and tradition. While we were filming in Gambia we talked at length with the second wife, who was worried about the fate of her husband's daughters. She had been willing to have the girls live with her and her husband, in an effort to save them.

The sad thing is, I can understand our driver's sense of powerlessness as a man. His first wife's sense of duty to tradition. His second wife's horror and disappointment. We are not talking about bad or evil people. Far from it. They are, however, trapped in a behavior that severely harms them.

It is from the perspective of our own contradictions as a society that we must seek to comprehend this grave problem faced by millions of our children and suffered by millions of our women. And suffered as well by men, who are by no means exempt from the self-inflicted wounding of the total society that mutilation ensures.

Warrior Marks is not a film about the virtues or the piteousness of victimhood. It was conceived, from the first, as a liberation film. These mutilations of body and spirit have occurred for from three to six thousand years. It is likely that they will continue well into the future, no matter what we do. That is why I try to focus on one child or one woman, when I think of the struggle ahead, instead of on all the millions who are at risk.

With this film, we, Pratibha Parmar and I, are sending a message to our sisters, millions of them yet unborn—and to our brothers who love them—and that message is this: If, in fact, you survive your mutilation, and the degradation that it imprints on soul and body, you still have a life to live. Live it with passion, live it with fierceness, live it with all the joy and laughter that you deserve.

Because your elders have told you that you are unclean does not make it so.

Because your mother has told you that you must hang your head in sorrow because you were born female does not make it so.

Because your father tells you he owns you body and soul and can do what he likes with you does not make it so.

Because your religion tells you there is a God who demands pieces of your flesh, and your perpetual suffering in sex and childbearing, does not mean this is *your* religion or *your* God.

We know that the women and children who suffer genital mutilation will have to stand up for themselves and, together, put an end to it. But that they need our help is indisputable.

What we can do is say: Out of our own suffering we can recognize yours.

Out of our own outrage, we join our voices to yours.

Out of our own self-respect, we affirm your right to be self-respecting and free from unwanted invasion or attack.

What can *you* do?

You can refrain from spending more than ten minutes stoning or attempting to malign the messenger. Within those minutes thousands of children will be mutilated. Your idle words will have the rumble of muffled screams beneath them.

You can study the situation and be informed, so that when there are children at risk in your own neighborhood, you will be aware of it.

You can make every effort to remember that it is the act of genital mutilation we wish to get rid of, not the people who do it, all of whom need our understanding and our love.

In that regard, I'd like to share the following about my encounter with the circumciser/mutilator whom you will see on the screen. The most daunting thing about confronting evil is that it tires you, and on the day that I was to interview her I was feeling really terrible. I had seen the young girls shuffling back to the village after having been mutilated ten days before. I had seen their sadness, the lack of light in their eyes. I'd also noted the arrogance of the circumciser/mutilator as she sought to convey to us a sense of her own importance. When I asked her what she felt when she cut the children and they screamed, and she said she never heard them, I felt chilled, even in that very hot climate. Still, as we talked, and as I was compelled to confront her incredible denial of the pain she constantly inflicts, I found myself completely *seeing* the old woman before me. And when I did—when I recognized the limitations of her life, the choices thrust upon her by her society, a society deadly to women; when I thought of her ignorance, deliberately enforced by the patriarchal nature of her culture—I felt all my anger, dread, and even my headache, draining away. I felt only compassion, which surprised me no end, and also, in a sense, saved me.

In my fifty years among African Americans I've noticed that, because of our suffering and our centuries-long insecurity, we have a hard time believing we are lovable. We also have a great fear of learning "bad" things about ourselves because we are sure these "bad" things will be cause for more people not to love us. I learned this decisively when there was so much controversy over *The Color Purple,* and there were actually people who thought that because I exposed incest and rape within the black community, I hated black men. In that situation, as in this, there is the fear of being left behind, of being abandoned, of having no one on your side, if all your "stuff" is exposed. This feeling, which is very deep with us, is understandable: it is a legacy of our having been stolen from or expelled by Africa and rejected, as human beings, by the EuroAmericans who enslaved us, and who set about undermining our language, our families, our bodily and mental integrity, and especially our sense of the Sacred.

Today, however, it is precisely compassionate love of ourselves and of others in which we must have faith. I have learned nothing about human beings that has stopped my loving them, and this is especially true of African and African-American human beings, who seem to me unsurpassed inspirers of affection, wonder, and love.

I ask you to have courage, as you watch *Warrior Marks,* not to fear knowing who we are, or what we have done to ourselves in the name of religion, male domination, female shame, or terrible ignorance.

All of us who worked to make this film welcome you to this encounter with the past and present that the film represents. *Warrior Marks* has been shown already in nine cities in the United States and abroad. Oakland is its tenth presentation. I have a special feeling about this screening because Oakland is home to so many

of the Bay Area's African Americans. I feel a special joy to be sharing it with you and with everyone else who has come to affirm
that it is the whole world today that is suffering, not just Africa,
and that what our suffering is teaching us is that it is much less if
we dare to encounter it together.

PART SIX

Saving the Self

Alice Walker holding Renée, a six-month-old refugee from El Salvador, prior to being arrested. Concord Naval Weapons Station, Concord, California. June 12, 1987.

PHOTOGRAPH BY BELVIE ROOKS

Getting as Black as My Daddy

THOUGHTS ON THE UNHELPFUL ASPECTS OF DESTRUCTIVE CRITICISM

Giving a Damn

Among the holiday cards I received this past Winter Solstice/Kwanza/Christmas season was one that depicted a large, naked Santa in an obscene position. It read: "Fuck You and Fuck Your Dead Mother." An assistant, who usually opens unsolicited mail, shrugged off my feeling of assault. "It's an impersonal message," said she, noting it had been typed on a computer. "This same message probably was sent to lots of people."

Still, it was addressed to me, and for at least an evening I was disturbed by it.

It symbolized for me the violent, hateful response to women's writing that has been part of my life, and that unfortunately has by now become a misogynist tradition around the world.

It reminded me of the verbal battering that so much of the criticism of black women's literary creations has become, and the ways in which even I am sometimes daunted in the face of such overt hostility. I say "even I" because one personal myth I've had is that I'm going to write just what I want to, anyhow, as a literary Bessie Smith or Billie Holiday might say, and just not give a damn.

Sometimes it's hard not to give a damn.

We needn't discuss the damage done to us all, as a community, when certain black male critics speak of black women writers, publicly, as "lesbians," "cunts," and "whores." (In a way that would make you think the three labels are synonymous.) Or of the prolonged, obviously psychotic fixations on particular black women writers that certain black male writers have displayed. I myself would not have dreamed of such insecurity in men who are, after all, literary creators themselves, often with considerable published work to their credit.

But looking at the card, and thinking about its message, I remembered the black woman critic who, writing in *The Village Voice* and *The Washington Post,* declared that although my political writing was banal, my writing about my spiritual development was simply of no interest. I believe the essay that most offended her, in my collection *Living by the Word,* was the one in which I connected the natural state of my hair to the natural state of the cosmos, and found it quite appropriate as an expression of the Universe's rich and inexhaustible creativity. I felt sorry for this critic, who could not accept my explorations and discoveries in the spirit in which I offered them—after all, what is truly banal is to think writers write books to please critics—but who instead chose to tell me she wished I'd shut up.

But this is not the worst part.

The worst part is that last summer I made a remarkable personal discovery about the wonders of my skin, and of color, and of colored people. I began writing about it, in an essay called "Getting as Black as My Daddy." Then I hesitated. Is this banal? I thought. Is it so personal as to be uninteresting? Why not shut up about it and keep my newfound and quite joyous discovery to myself? I would simply keep the title, which I liked and which I pasted to the side of my computer, and the face of my very dark brown father in a safe and liberated section of my soul.

I realize as I write this that mentioning this unwritten essay is a sneaky way of "writing" it. And since I am aware of this, I might as well tell you some of the particulars.

I end the essay here, not telling you the particulars, as a demonstration of what, because of battering rather than constructive criticism, is sometimes lost.

Comments written for, but not delivered to, the Black Women's Health Collective (Atlanta, Georgia).

This Side of Glory

THE AUTOBIOGRAPHY OF DAVID HILLIARD AND THE STORY OF THE BLACK PANTHER PARTY
BY DAVID HILLIARD AND LEWIS COLE

Saving the Self

People who experienced the Sixties and the Black Panther Party in the Bay Area should read *This Side of Glory* by David Hilliard and Lewis Cole and share its meaning with their children. Like Elaine Brown's *A Taste of Power,* it is one of recent history's most jarring records. Elaine Brown's book tells what it was like to be a bold, brilliant, ambitious black woman in the party, giving orders when she briefly becomes leader—while Huey Newton is in exile in Cuba—and therefore experiencing "a taste of power," but at other times using her sexuality and being used sexually by the men in the party because that is a way she can connect with an unknown father—a cruel and superciliously bourgeois father, as it turns out—and convince her comrades she is still "just a woman." She writes of being "disciplined" by a gathering of "brothers," one of whom wields a bullwhip against her bare back. Nor is this the only instance of one of slavery's strongest institutions, public flogging, being perpetuated by "revolutionaries" who denounce black people's enslavement by whites at every turn.

Hilliard's book pays minimal, if obligatory, attention to the role of women in the party. Hilliard was Huey Newton's oldest and best friend among party members; they had met when Hilliard, recently arrived in Oakland from Alabama with his family, was eleven. They became extremely close, eventually sharing, as Hilliard writes, money, drugs, and women. They bonded so tightly, in fact, that Hilliard became addicted to Huey's intelligence, beauty, and charisma and could barely manage a thought or emotion that was purely his own. He had this problem to a lesser degree with Eldridge Cleaver, the political chameleon who, in both Hilliard's and Brown's books, comes off as the psychotic opportunist many contemporaries took him to be. In fact, as Hilliard tells it, it was Cleaver's action as provocateur that led to the death of Lil' Bobby Hutton, a young idealistic Panther who idolized his elders and for whom many of the older men felt responsible, in a shootout with an overwhelmingly better-armed police force. Cleaver is also partly blamed for the subsequent hammering away at the party by police and FBI agents enraged by his highly inflammatory and militaristic rhetoric.

All of these men abused women, and apparently thought little about it. Kathleen Cleaver was beaten by Eldridge. Huey had women beaten and was charged with the shooting death of a seventeen-year-old who was selling her body to make a living. She allegedly called him a punk. Hilliard harasses a woman he likes until he forces her to go out with him. Marries her. "Fights" with her. Cheats on her. Has children by another woman. All along demonstrating more loyalty to Huey Newton than to the two women together.

It isn't really fear of the police or the FBI that drives the men in the Black Panther Party. Panthers regularly, almost routinely, stand these "pigs" down or shoot it out with them. They absorb devastating losses from vicious police raids and murders. J. Edgar Hoover declares the Black Panthers the greatest internal threat to American security, and all the force of the United States government is unleashed against them. They are effectively, from a "military" point of view, destroyed. It is the charge of being a punk that sends each and every one of these warriors into conniptions. "Punk" is what Huey calls Eldridge as he expels him from the party—a charge so threatening that the usually glib and politically garrulous Cleaver is struck dumb.

These were men who loved, admired, and were sometimes in love with, each other. They were confused by this. Who, at the time, after all, except perhaps James Baldwin, could have taught them that love is *the* revolutionary emotion, partly because it cannot be limited, cannot be compartmentalized, cannot be controlled. But of course Baldwin, by Cleaver's definition, was a punk. They were also men who grew up without fathers, or with extremely distant, remote, inaccessible ones. Men who learned about manhood from white men pursuing fake justice and bogus law and order on television. They might, like Hilliard, adore their mothers, but they dared not emulate or identify with her strengths: love of family, devotion to kin and mates, patience with children, humble service to the community. To do so would make them sissies. Sissies grow up to be punks. Each man—Hilliard, Cleaver, Newton, as well as Stokely Carmichael, always obviously distant from himself—felt empty and alone. When they met each other, counterparts and equals, it was a case of being smitten on sight. The homoeroticism in Hilliard's carefully worded memories of Huey is so evident as to be comic. For one thing, Newton always seems caught in the act of disrobing. Then again, he spends much of his time thinking aloud in or speaking from his bed. He manages to sleep not only with Hilliard's girlfriend, Brenda, but with his wife, Pat. He insists that Brenda spend the night with him on days she's visited Hilliard in prison. In this same habit of sharing "substances" and women's bodies rather than their own souls, Hilliard introduces Newton to crack.

Most interesting of all perhaps is Huey's response to the famous photograph of himself seated like a warrior king in a large wicker chair, beret cocked to the side, legs slightly spread, a confident tilt to his handsome head, a gun in one hand, a spear in the other. He detested the photograph. Everyone else loved it. He said this photograph wasn't him. Perhaps he recognized it for the pinup it was. It enraged him that Eldridge Cleaver had taken the photograph and that this unreal Huey—a punk with revolutionary style—was Cleaver's view of him. A view accepted, subliminally, by warriors and masses alike.

Did these men, many of them imprisoned for long periods of time, ever have sexual relationships with other men? It's a question that presents itself. And if they did, does this account for the overreaction to the charge of being a punk? And the desperate need to demonstrate "manhood" even when it led to death? Would it account, perhaps, for the profound emptiness each man felt in the presence of families dutifully if absentmindedly constructed. Abusing "their" women, neglecting their children (Hilliard's son robbed people from an early age, just for fun, and became a drug dealer and user along with his father and mother), feeling purposeful and energetic only in the frenzied acts of resistance and solidarity that seemed best enjoyed in the company of other men.

When Huey Newton rejected Hilliard as well as the party itself and saturated himself with the dust of cocaine and the fumes of crack, what was he running from? An image of himself created by a man he didn't trust, an image the people expected to come to life? An image Newton knew was false? Or one he feared might be all too true? When David Hilliard's life became one of constant searching for the next "rock" to smoke, what was *he* running from? Perhaps from the unbearable fact that in losing Huey—to drugs and paranoia long before Huey's murder—he lost not only a childhood friend and comrade but also a lover, whether or not they ever made love.

In any event, these Black Panther brothers lived far from their true natures. They were not black panthers after all, cool and distant and sleek, but vulnerable black men whose fight against injustice, because it turned violent beyond their wildest nightmares, moved them further and further from the gentleness and humor that once, no doubt, were their core. Living far from one's nature is not unusual in our culture, which is why the drug conquest of America is virtually complete. If you do not have your own self as your essence, you will fill the void with anything you can, from alcohol and other drugs to women (or men) and revolution, but it will still not be you. And far from leading "the people" to a clearer understanding of themselves, you will lead them only into a deeper, more cynical, and more humiliating confusion.

Revolution really must occur within. It is this that David Hilliard begins to learn when he joins an AA program after he and his wife have been reduced to living in abandoned cars, attempting to kill each other over drugs. This book is, amazingly, a belated Panther triumph, not because David Hilliard, former chief of staff of the Black Panther Party has found a way to save the masses, as the Panthers in their best moments wanted to do, but because he at last understands the value of saving the self.

A severely edited version of this essay appeared in The New York Times *as an op-ed piece in 1993.*

Disinformation Advertising

Diet Sprite and Spaghetti Sauce

One day a friend asked me whether I'd ever done an advertisement for Ford, the automobile manufacturer. "I don't even *like* Fords!" I said, laughing.

"Don't laugh," she said, handing me a clipping a friend of hers had sent her. Indeed, it was a full-page profile of me, complete with photograph, with the Ford logo and the word "Advertisement" emblazoned across the top. It had been torn from the pages of *New Woman* magazine. Attached to it was a letter from a woman who asked: "What does this ad mean? It appears as though Alice Walker was paid several thousand dollars to make a Ford promotion look good. . . . Does this mean writers with her success and status will someday be on television advertising diet Sprite or spaghetti sauce?"

I was stunned.

I had nothing whatsoever to do with this ad, had never been asked for permission to use my image or career to advance Ford's corporate cause, and furthermore have never, to this day, driven a Ford.

I immediately sent off a letter of protest to the magazine, and letters to my attorney and agent requesting they do something about this ad, which misrepresented me. Not, ironically, in its content—which tended to praise my accomplishments—but in its presentation of my life and image under the logo of a corporation to whom I had not given permission and about which I know little. All I *do* know about Ford is that the truck, to me, has always symbolized perfectly the dominant white male American culture: blunt, boxy, powerful, and square.*

When I first read the letter that asked whether I and other "successful" writers would soon be touting diet Sprite and spaghetti sauce, I was annoyed by the writer's assumption that I was complicit in the creation of the ad. What have I ever done, I fumed, that would lead anyone to think I would sink so low as to endorse an automobile company? But then I remembered hearing a black man say on television that he would do a commercial for the Ku Klux Klan for five million dollars, the sum Michael Jackson had apparently been paid to endorse a soft drink. Even as I watched the words leave his mouth I couldn't believe it. But there they were. How, in fact, *is* a reader to know that there are writers and artists whose images and lives are not for sale to corporate giants?

May I suggest that if you, dear reader, should ever come across an ad that makes you wonder about the person being presented, do exactly what my friend's friend did: bring it to the attention of the person involved. *This is important*. Because I don't read magazines regularly, I had no way of knowing about the Ford ad unless someone told me about it. It is true that you may find writers who actually do endorse Ford and other corporations, but my guess is that the writers you assume would not do so, don't. Address the writer in care of his or her publisher, clip the offending article or ad, and send it along. I fear we are in for another long period of disinformation in the United States, and some of it will probably be extremely subtle. (For example, when I showed one friend the ad,

---

* In fairness to Ford, some of their small contemporary trucks I like very much.

he couldn't see why I was so upset, since everything said in it was complimentary.) As women and people of color and white activist men, we will have to keep our faith in one another strong. Question everything that seems strange or wrong to you concerning the mainstream presentation of your allies. It is better to annoy a writer by alerting her or him to erroneous "news" than to let it percolate unrefuted in the community, to the detriment of the writer *and* the community.

I am not saying that everyone has the time, energy, or finances to refute every lie or distortion that appears, but perhaps from time to time we can, individually or collectively, communicate a general indication of where we stand.

UPDATE: *New Woman* and Ford apologized. *New Woman* agreed to publish a statement in a future issue admitting it ran the ad without my knowledge or permission. Ford offered a monetary settlement, which was donated to two of my favorite activist organizations: The Color Purple Education Foundation of Eatonton, Georgia (the money to be used to teach children to swim), and The Ms. Foundation for Women of New York, to assist feminist publishing.

Letter to the International Indian Treaty Council

Sacred "Moons"

San Francisco, California
November 29, 1989
Dear Friends:

I am writing to let you know that I believe your custom of segregating menstruating women from others during religious (and other) ceremonies is wrong, hurtful to solidarity, and historically unsound.

The very first societies, cultures, and civilizations, all over the world, were founded by women. Because men and women alike were known to be created out of women's blood, menstrual blood itself was sacred. These matristic (mother-centered) societies were violently overthrown by men, who then instituted societies dominated by men.

My partner, Robert Allen, and I came to Alcatraz because we wanted to acknowledge the true meaning of Thanksgiving.* To recognize the near-miraculous survival, against incredible odds, of

---

* Alcatraz Island in San Francisco Bay was formerly the site of a federal prison. After the prison was closed in 1963, Native Americans "reclaimed" the island. Each year on Thanksgiving Day a ceremony commemorating Native American culture and Native American resistance to European American domination is held—an "un-Thanksgiving."

native peoples all over the earth, and to take our stand, as human beings, against any form of man-made separation, segregation, and apartheid.

We chose to sit with the menstruating women to express our solidarity with the first people of all cultures oppressed because of physical difference—women.

The male-instigated and -imposed "tradition" of excluding women from religious services is the same in the overwhelming majority of patriarchal cultures in the world. Native Americans, like African Americans and African AmerIndians, are not exempt from this poisonous divisiveness that has weakened our tribes and made all our judgments psychologically lopsided because they represent male views only. It is well known that menstruating women express their true feelings more honestly during their "moons" than at any other time. It is because of this, I believe, that men originally banished them. To exclude menstruating women from ceremonies and councils is one way of silencing woman's voice, and losing the benefit of her judgment. And where has this led us? To a world run by men whose highest expression of emotion regularly culminates in violence and destruction. Whereas archaeologists have now proven that matristic societies were universally characterized by their peacefulness, over thousands of years.

I hope you will consider what I am saying very carefully. We are in for times of unusual toughness, when our wholehearted solidarity with one another as oppressed people will be crucial. I know that as a woman, I reserve the right to decide when and whether I will participate in events to which, after all, I have been invited. To ask me to do otherwise is not to honor me as a woman, or as a person.

In struggle,
Alice Walker

Letter to People for the Ethical Treatment of Animals

Dear Friends:

I am pleased to submit the following statement on horses and the Premarin* issue:

> Horses are some of the most beautiful creatures Nature has devised. They are a symbol to us of all that is graceful, fluid, and free. Our Souls need them.
>
> To imprison pregnant mares in order to use their urine to make Premarin, an estrogen-replacement drug for menopausal women, is an outrage against nature and beauty that will inevitably be felt by the women to whom this drug is administered.

* The name Premarin is derived from "pregnant mares' urine." Horses are artificially impregnated, their urine is collected, and estrogen is extracted from it. The mares are forced to be pregnant most of their lives. Their offspring are taken away at birth.

We are not spiritually unconnected from the drugs we take, nor from the pain and suffering that goes into their making.

One's life cannot ultimately be improved because a mother mare must give up her child to a dog-food company, while she herself must stand for seven months in a stall too small to turn around in.

Menopausal women of the world unite! There is always an alternative to cruelty.

For there to be a future at all, grandmothers must show the way. Be strong in the face of natural transitions. Remember that the horse grows large and strong by eating plants. Menopausal women can get all the estrogen they need from the same source.

Sincerely,
Alice Walker

Follow Me Home

Written and directed
by Peter Bratt

Few American films, past or present, are as important and powerful as *Follow Me Home,* Native American Peter Bratt's debut film, whose central meditation is how we relate to our ancestral and present-day selves; and how, consciously accepting the experience and wisdom of those who've gone before, we relate to each other. It is a work that explores issues of societal and planetary survival: the meaning of integrity, the uses of memory, the courage required by love, and the necessity of respect.

The film opens on a discussion among four male friends: Tudee and Abel, Chicano cousins; Kaz, an African American; and Freddy, a Native American, as they, together, paint a large, colorful mural on the side of an urban building. It soon becomes clear that they are planning a journey: to drive across the country, from East Los Angeles to Washington, D.C., and to paint a mural on the White House. There is much hope in their quite funny dialogue about the trip. There is trepidation too.

For, as Tudee says: "Cause you know, brothers, This ain't gonna be no Sunday stroll. After all, we're talking about going to Washington, D.C., and painting the White House. Putting our colors and our images on the walls of La Casa Blanca."

Each of the men understands the symbolic power of such an event, aware that it is only when we can paint our own vivid dreams on the white blankness of the nation's canvas that we have a chance of bringing them, and ourselves, to life. The White House, in particular, has been a symbol of oppression to subjugated peoples of color since it was constructed during the colonial period; transforming it into a colorful expression of the presence of American people of color as we approach the next century (perhaps leaving one side of it white, as an example of fair representation) is a cheerful ambition in itself.

All is not smooth sailing, however, even within the group. On a stop before leaving L.A. and *el barrio,* Abel, the most hardened of the men, picks up a gun from a local bodega clerk in exchange for a few rocks of crack. From this point in the film, we understand that the long ride to Washington, D.C., is destined to be a bumpy one. That "the man" they expect to encounter in the White House does not represent the only problem.

As the van, owned by Freddy, rattles along the back roads of middle America, we learn of other demons harassing the minds and spirits of the passengers. Freddy is in recovery from a drinking problem; Tudee is planning to sell, as solely his own work, paintings that are the product of the group. Abel can't read, and can express himself only through vile language and violent behavior; Kaz is struggling to define himself outside the narrow stereotype of "black dude" in which society, and even Abel, attempt to encage him.

In one of the most startling scenes in the film, the four men encounter Evey, an African-American woman traveling alone. She carries a mysterious package and seems to be in a state of shock. Evey is played with intense vulnerability and realness by Alfre Woodard. Because of a bizarre accident on the road, in which a white man dressed as an Indian is killed, Evey joins the men in the van, her amazing and painful story connecting with theirs.

This is a journey, we discover, primarily toward our own selves. A journey to discover who we still are, after all these years of the most devastating humiliation, subjugation, enslavement, and eradi-cation. Who and what are the Spirits still caring about us? How do we as artists continue to make ourselves worthy of the ancestors' trust? How do we as human beings make ourselves whole enough to deserve the respect and love of each other, especially when there is so much bad history, so much fear?

Art unfailingly reflects its creator's heart. Art that comes from a heart open to all the possible paths there might be to a healthier tomorrow cannot help but be medicine for the tribe. In *Follow Me Home* we see ourselves in our shame and our joy. We see that self-love is the medicine we have most often left on the shelf. We see that this need not continue to be so. We see that we can move toward each other, and not run away in terror. We have ancestors in common who have already done this: run toward, and embraced, each other. We see, in fact, that the spirits we have hon-ored and loved, both in our histories and in ourselves, have not yet deserted us.

Letter to the Editor of *Essence*

Second submittal, December 5, 1990

Being Kin to Seaweed, Bushy Plants, and Trees

Dear Editor:

Two fairly recent comments about dreadlocks in your magazine have stayed on my mind: one, that beginning dreadlocks must not be washed for three months(!), in an article about how one acquires locks; the other, that "dreadlocks smell," quoted from the book of a black woman who had obviously been sniffing the unwashed dreadlocks aforementioned. Though I have written at some length about my own experience of wearing dreadlocks—in an essay called "Oppressed Hair Puts a Ceiling on the Brain," in *Living by the Word*—I've felt compelled to offer these further comments.

Though some people may start their dreadlocks by not washing their hair for three months, this is by no means the only way. My daughter has dreadlocks, my best friends, male and female, have dreadlocks, and none of us has ever gone more than a week or so between hairwashings. I find it hard to imagine anyone going for such a long time with unwashed hair, though I've met one woman who said she used a kind of cleaning oil instead of water. I regret that the writer of your article was unaware that one of the main reasons people dread is because they can wash their hair frequently, since worrying about losing one's hairstyle or having one's hair "go back" (if one uses hot combs or perms) becomes a thing of the past. Undoubtedly there will be readers of your magazine who feel that three months of heavy, dirty hair is too high a price to pay for any kind of eventual freedom, and who can blame them? However, to give up the possibility of dreading is, I think, to miss one of the primary liberating experiences of one's life as a black person. Permitting one's hair to grow as long and as wildly as it likes in its natural state is an unexcelled spiritual and political expression and a sweetly self-loving and rebelliously *gentle* pleasure.

Generally speaking, dreadlocks that are washed smell great. Many people with dreadlocks live, or try to live, a clean and natural lifestyle. Their hair is washed with soap or shampoo that has only natural ingredients. There seems to be a fondness for coconut oil shampoo, sweet almond conditioner, or other cleansers made of herbs and flowers. There is never a smell of lye or peroxide or of any of the dangerous carcinogenic chemicals found in hair straighteners: chemicals that are just as bad for the environment, since they eventually find their way into our rivers and reservoirs and drinking water, as they are, psychologically, for our spirits, as we admit, each time we face the mirror, that the persons who control our hair ultimately control our image, and to a large extent, therefore, control us.

It is truly enlightening, in this regard, to view the contentment and calm self-respect exhibited by children whose parents have lovingly allowed them to wear their natural hair, and to contrast this with the behavior of those who have the oppressed demeanor of little people who've never known what they look like. And who are therefore always rearranging themselves, futilely, in an attempt to look like somebody else.

Some people start their locks by simply not combing their hair. Some people tie off sections with strings. Some people braid their hair, let it grow out, then snip off the braided ends (which I did).

Some people simply twist their hair into curls until the curls "lock." (This is what my daughter and our friends did.) The "locking," by the way, is what happens when the kinks in our hair knit. This happens naturally, and it is one reason why, when people ask me, "What do you have to do to have dreadlocks?" my response is "Have at least one African ancestor." But the washing of the hair continues, throughout.

It is also erroneous to think dreadlocks are the same hair forever. Although the hair seems to grow faster and longer than it would in any other style, there is a lot of shedding of old hair. It simply comes off, occasionally, in one's hand. Or, every six months or so, while sitting around listening to music with dreaded friends, someone will offer to snip off a couple of inches. The only problem I've ever noted with dreadlocks is their tendency to hold lint, but this can be dealt with simply by bending from the waist, sweeping one's locks over one's head, and giving them a vigorous batting with one's hands. Angela Davis, who has the most splendid locks imaginable, once showed me that this is also a good method for speedy drying, as well as excellent exercise for the waist, upper arms, hands, and neck.

I am aware that many people dislike the name "dreadlocks" because they assume "dread" itself is a negative word. Not to mention the word "locks." I like, even enjoy, the word "dreadlocks" because whenever I use it I find myself in bemused dialogue with African ancestors on several continents—those of our people who grew to dislike their own hair because its uniqueness was unappreciated by the flat-haired people who conquered them and who decreed their own physical characteristics the norm. Glancing in a dictionary created by these conquerors, one finds, indeed: "dread 1. to fear greatly; be in extreme apprehension of: *to dread death;* 2. to be reluctant to do, meet, experience: *I dread going to big parties.*" However, it is the *archaic* description, "3. to hold in respectful awe," that comes closest to the way I personally feel about black people's hair, because it really is such an amazing expression. Not unlike certain kinds of seaweed, bushy plants, or trees. As for "locks," *Web-*

ster's defines it: "1. a tress or portion of hair; 2. *locks,* the hair of the head; 3. a flock or small portion of wool, cotton, flax, etc." (all of which our natural hair resembles). Related to the Dutch word "lok," meaning "curl."

My one concern in writing this is that readers will assume I am proselytizing. I am not. Like everything else, dreading is not for everyone. My only interest is that such a healthful, natural experience be given justice, and that the truth be told about it, to the extent that this is possible. My daughter and I have noticed some interesting things, though, about people who dread. For instance, when one's naturally generous flow of energy is blocked by anger, hatred, or self-condemnation, locks will not grow. All the more reason, it is clear to us, that each head must make its own decision about how it will appear. Not for nothing does every person's hair lie so close to the brain.

Alice Walker
Northern California

POSTSCRIPT: This letter was not printed by *Essence.* A year or so later, without my knowledge or permission, parts of it appeared in the magazine in another writer's article about hair and the variety of ways to wear it, including fried.

African Cinema

Taking My Little-Girl Self Back to the Movies

I recall with sadness my first experiences of cinema. Nowhere were there characters who reminded me of myself; nowhere reflections of the beloved or puzzling faces of family or community members. Only extremely pale white people—committing robberies, murders, marriage, and mayhem—dashed or struggled across the screen; and, in fact, they did not often resemble the whites of my small Southern town either. Everyone in the theater, whites in their section downstairs, blacks in the gallery upstairs, enjoyed Westerns; enjoyed scenes depicting the destruction of the Indian nations and the triumph of "civilization" over nature. They also enjoyed films that depicted the cowardice and lack of intelligence of Africans, shown innumerable times in mumbling, knee-knocking, head-scratching subservience to whatever white male actor was playing Tarzan at the time. How it hurts, today, to acknowledge the amount of poison that was being poured into my little girl's brain.

It is with joy, then, that I encourage you to view the films presented in the Library of African Cinema. These are moving, sincere films, fully engaged with their culture, created by filmmakers who have made every attempt to be true to the character and personhood of their people. The Africa in these films is an authentic presence. The Africans are holy, flawed, sane, crazy, confused, loving, daring, worried, competent, a mess—just as they exist. And, true to the African landscape and organization of traditional life depicted in several of the films, there is even a different sense of time from that experienced in Western films, which works mesmerizingly on the viewer, so that at the end of a film such as *Yeelen* one almost feels one has been in Africa during several centuries. It is rewarding as well to see in these films a substantial degree of consciousness regarding such contemporary concerns as the rights of women, in *Finzan;* the struggle against apartheid, in *Mapantsula;* and the inherent danger, to people and the environment, of mindless urbanization and dictatorship, explored in one of my personal favorites, *Zan Boko.* A sign of any satisfying experience is the wish to repeat it. I have watched several of these films more than once, with pride that African filmmakers work so hard to restore us to ourselves, as adults, and with the feeling that at last I am able to offer my little-girl self an antidote to her pain.

Amandla! The power is ours!, I think you will say when you've viewed these films. Because, really, it is.

I Am Salman Rushdie

*A statement read at a gathering of writers
in San Francisco, protesting the threat
to the life of Salman Rushdie.*

Standing Where We Can

It has been hard to sleep since I heard about the threat against Salman Rushdie's life. I toss and turn at night, thinking about what he must be feeling. To know there are millions of people focused on the taking of his life, and for something he did simply as an expression of his being—for good writers write what they believe; they cannot help it—must be an indescribably ugly sensation. He must feel as if his heart has fallen through his shoes.

The world is forced to suffer this with Rushdie, for even those who hate him and would accept the five million pieces of silver for his death are yoked to his life, to these anxious, pain-filled days, by a frenzy they neither devised nor can control.

What does it feel like to have a mob screaming for your life?

On these past sleepless nights, an old memory that I had put away came back again. Of an evening, just at dusk, during my student days, while I was working in the human rights movement in the South. Of a sit-in on the porch of the Georgia Highway Patrol in Liberty County, Georgia; and of a mob of white supremacists who threw rocks and bottles and foul language at me, and at the women and men and small children who had joined our protest. At the time I did not seem to feel the terror. Only now, as my heart plunges to my own shoes at what this new kind of censorship of creative people may let loose in the world, do I remember that, in fact, it was something beyond terror that I felt. I felt grief—intense, piercing—to see people so mad, so hopelessly misinformed, so manipulatively deranged. They actually felt, at the time, that by expressing a need to be black and free, in a society constructed by white supremacists to serve their own racist ends, I was insulting everything they stood for: their ancestors, their religion, their "Southern Way of Life," the sanctity of their white skin itself.

I am glad I have learned a bit about the Moors, who, in the centuries they inhabited Spain, interpreted Islam as a religion tolerant of diverse ideas; dedicated to free expression and to learning, even for women. And I can't help but think of Malcolm X, such a devout Muslim, such a brave man. And such a fearless follower of his own mind. Where would he stand today?

Well, I have lived long enough to know we stand where we can. It's the only way we will ever get any sleep.

This That I Offer You

People Get Tired; Sometimes They Have Other Things to Do

Over the twenty-five years of my writing and publishing life I've been amazed to find myself appearing, usually recognizable only by my name, in the thoughts, fantasies, words, and even marketing strategies of others. Perhaps this is a price one pays for being a figure the public feels it knows. Men I've never seen in my life have claimed in print that we've lunched together *and that I flirted*. Men and women I don't know swear they were my best friends or close relatives when we were growing up; now they want money, a job or school recommendation, and a hug. Not long ago I opened the newspaper to a story in which a well-known black male writer complained that he'd come up to speak to me in an airport somewhere and I'd ignored him. This is a man I've seen exactly twice, both times in poor light, ten and fifteen years ago respectively. We have never had a conversation. The headline actually said, in big black letters: "ALICE WALKER STILL HASN'T FORGIVEN HIM." Forgiven him? I don't even remember him. Which is to say, like the majority of readers in the country, I recognize his name, not his face.

Recently, sadly, I've been alternately irritated and puzzled by Anna Caday's* various accounts of feeling "shunned" by me and by her incredible need, apparently, for my ————. The blank is there because I cannot imagine what it is she needs. Here is a woman whose books are selling spectacularly. (Perhaps Toni Morrison and I had some small role in this, herstorically speaking.) She is witty, poised, attractive. People like her and appreciate her work. She has lots of money. A child. Friends. Her health. Her cup, in short, runneth over. And yet I find in *Essence,* as in *The New York Times* and even in *The Times* of London, that with all this, she still needs something from me and from Toni Morrison. What can it possibly be?

Just as *Patience and Stress*† began its triumphant march across the country I sent Caday a note congratulating her on its success. It is true I refused to talk to the rude reporter from *The New York Times* who later wrote an article about Caday—titled, gauchely, I thought, "Caday's Carats"—not only because I had yet to read the book but because he was obnoxious. He seemed offended that I would refuse to be interviewed by someone from the *Times* simply because I had nothing to say. Each of the three or four times he called (driving my assistant to ever higher levels of exasperation) he'd concocted yet another reason for my refusal. One of them, as I recall, was that he "guessed" I didn't want to help another black woman writer. Since I have a respectable record to stand on in this regard, I dismissed him as the uninformed novice he obviously was.

If Ms. Caday wrote more than one note to me—she says in an article that she'd "done everything" to get a response from me and Toni Morrison—I haven't seen it. Sending galleys of her books to me for blurbs isn't different from the "everything" done by hundreds of other writers.

The context for the infamous "shunning" episode was as follows. At a reading of my children's book *Finding the Green Stone* (I

---

* Not her real name.
† Not its real title.

had met Ms. Caday a few weeks earlier at a signing for the same book), she asked me to talk about the subject of my coming book *Possessing the Secret of Joy*. Because my audience was mostly children three to twelve years old, I felt it inappropriate to talk about the novel's subject: the devastating effects on women and children of genital mutilation. I declined to comment. Later, as I was signing books, Ms. Caday came up and said, "I'm Anna Caday," as if this fact, had I known it, might have changed my decision. "I know," I said. She said, "I just wanted people to know about your book." I said, "They will know about it soon enough." Considering the subject matter of the novel, its implications for all our children and for Africa, this was said more in sadness—I may even have groaned—than in pique.

What can we do about the needs others have of us that we, being human and therefore limited and imperfect, cannot fulfill? I have thought about this for a long time, and now, as an elder—well, approaching that status—I wish to tell a tale of a time when I myself might have come close to feeling, as Ms. Caday seems to, rejected or ignored.

Once upon a time, when I was in my early twenties, I met the great human being and writer Langston Hughes. It was love at first sight, I believe, for both of us. I saw in him a loving father/uncle. He saw in me a worshipful daughter/niece. Having no one else to turn to at the time, I used to write to Langston. He wrote back. Until one day, just when I needed him most, he failed to answer a letter I had written and sent off rather urgently. Many things went through my mind: that he really didn't like me, after all; that my letters bored him; that somehow I'd angered or disappointed him; that he didn't think my short story that he'd agreed to anthologize was any good; that maybe, like many black men of the time, he disapproved of the Jewish law student I'd decided to marry. And on and on and on. I saw myself very large, in fact, in Langston's mind.

A week or so went by. One day I received a letter with his return address but not written in his wonderful bright-green ink. I opened it with a troubled heart. Langston Hughes had died, I was informed, before receiving my letter, but the writer knew he had thought highly of me. This was an invitation to his funeral.

We must learn to accept, as I had to then, that people get tired, cross, overworked, and overextended. They go out of the country just when you write to them, and may be gone for months. If they are well known, they get more stuff in the mail than they can possibly read or respond to. They have love affairs from which they refuse to emerge to talk shop. They get PMS. Or, in Langston's case, prostate cancer. They get sick and sometimes they die. And none of it has anything, really, to do with us, and what we need or expect from them. Langston's death taught me this, just as his caring but firmly self-respecting manner is something I have wished to emulate and to bring into all conflicts I have with people, especially those of color. It is this that I offer you.

PART SEVEN

Hugging Fidel

Kathy Engle, Alice Walker, Pratibha Parmar, Leslie Kagan, Fidel Castro Ruz, Angela Davis, Rachel Cohen, at the Palacio de la Revolución, Havana, Cuba. September, 1995.

PHOTOGRAPH BY A <u>COMPAÑERA</u>, USING PRATIBHA'S CAMERA.

Becoming What We're Called

"Boy, Man, Fellow, Chap"

Last night, before I could stop myself, I put my arms around a dear friend who'd just said she'd see us later, "you guys!" and told her I don't like being called "guy." In fact, I told her, noting her puzzled expression, I detest it.

I remember once, many years ago, attending a spring festival in the seaside village of this same friend. The air was scented with early flowers, the sun was shining brightly off the ocean. My friend found a table for us not far from the grill on which hot dogs and tofu burgers were being flipped. Within minutes, unbeckoned, three teenage maidens brought us overflowing platters of food, freshly prepared, lovingly arranged, a feast. One was brown-haired, one blond, and one as redheaded as the daughter of my next-hill-over neighbors, who was named after the Irish Goddess Bridget. I suppose it was partly this that caused me to think of the three young women, so solicitous, so gracefully nurturing, as Goddesses. Thanking them, I was just about to comment on the Goddess nature of their behavior when my friend said cheerfully, "Thank you, you guys!" I felt they had not been seen, that their essential nature had been devalued, but I said nothing, not wanting to offend my friend.

Sometimes I think these struggles about identity will never end; this one reminds me of nothing so much as of the battle black people seem to have lost a decade ago against the word "nigger." Seeking to redeem it, to render it harmless, many people deliberately kept it alive among themselves. Now, because of rap, it is commonplace to hear it bouncing through the air, no matter where you are, and if you are not fond of it, you feel all the assault such a negative description brings. (*Nigger:* a vulgar, offensive term of hostility and contempt, as used by Negrophobes.) Recently, for instance, two other friends and I were walking through the San Francisco Botanical Garden, the only black people there, the only black women. It is crucial, living in the city, to have access to nature: a place where you can relax, be yourself, and relate to the magnificence of the earth without thinking every moment of life in a racist, violent society. We stood by a pond on which there were hundreds of birds and marveled at the way the fluttering of their wings stirred the air. It was a beautiful day. The sun was warm, the sky blue, the Asian magnolias in full expression. Suddenly, out of nowhere, it seemed, we heard, very loud, "black nigger black . . . dah, dah, dah." We looked about for the racist white man who had dared shatter our peace. He was not there. Instead, the retreating back of a young black man, bopping in tune to music from his Walkman, told the story. He was singing along with someone whose refrain, "black nigger black," he echoed. We watched as he swung along, oblivious to the beauty all around him, his attention solely on this song. He went the length of the garden, seeing nothing; only thinking of how he was black and a nigger and this was all the identity he had. It was like watching him throw mud, or worse, all over himself.

I have asked people, both men and women, why they like "you guys." Some admit they picked it up from a television commercial that seemed cute to them. Others add, incredibly, that they felt it was an all-inclusive term for males and females; they considered it gender free. Some recalled the expression "guys and gals" and said, laughing, nobody wanted to be "gals." I tried to imagine everyone in American calling themselves and each other "you gals." How many men would accept it? Personally, for gender-free inclusivity, I prefer the Southern expression "you all."

After the completion of *Warrior Marks,* a film we made about female genital mutilation, Pratibha Parmar and I premiered it in ten European and American cities, an exhausting but at times exhilarating tour. But after about the third city, we realized that the most exhausting thing was neither the travel nor the stress we experienced as we anticipated each audience's response to the film; it was having, at every theater, to endure the following questions: How long did it take "you guys" to do this? What was it like for "you guys" to travel and film in Africa? The women asking us these questions seemed blind to us, and in their blindness we felt our uniqueness as female creators disappear. We had recently been in societies where some or all of a woman's genitalia were forcibly cut from her by other women who collaborated—wholeheartedly, by now—with men. To us, the refusal to acknowledge us as women seemed a verbal expression of this same idea. It made us quite ill. After all, it would have been impossible for "guys" to make the film we had made. No women would have talked to them, for one thing. Each night, over and over, we told the women greeting us: We are not "guys." We are women. Many failed to get it. Others were amused. One woman amused *us,* she had so much difficulty not saying "you guys," every two minutes, even after we'd complained!

It would seem from the dictionary that the verb "guy" is another word for "guide," or "control": bearing a very real resemblance to "husband." It means "to steady, stay, or direct by means of a guy, from the French *guying.*" The noun means "a boy or man; fellow; chap." It means "a person whose appearance or dress is odd." Again, as a verb, "guy" can mean "to tease; to ridicule." And this last is how I feel it when the word is used by men referring to women, and by women referring to themselves. I see in its use some women's obsequious need to be accepted at any cost, even at the cost of erasing their own femaleness, and that of other women. Isn't it at least ironic that after so many years of struggle for women's liberation, women should end up calling themselves this?

I think my friend is probably exasperated with me because of what I said to her last night. After all, "you guys" is a habitual expression in conversation around the world; I am asking her not to call me something that comes easily, apparently, to her. I think perhaps I am a trying friend to have; one who wonders, as I can't help but do, why this should be so. The magic of naming is that people often become what they are called. What in me evokes this word from her? I will call her up in a day or two and suggest we go for a walk and discuss this issue in the open arena of nature, where the larkspur is not called delphinium and the hummingbird is not labeled dove. Grass is not called tree and rocks are not called bears. When I look at her I see a black woman daily overcoming incredible odds to live a decent, honest, even merry life. Someone who actively nurtures community wherever she goes. Someone who has raised a strong daughter and now showers affection and attention on a beautiful grandchild. I see someone who dances like a Nubian and cooks like a Creole. I don't respect "guys" enough to obliterate the woman that I see by calling her by their name.

The Story of Why I Am Here

or A Woman Connects Oppressions

An address given at a Peace for Cuba Rally,
February 1, 1992, the birthday of Langston Hughes,
who, like Hemingway, loved Cuba.

Putting My Arms Around Sadie Hussein, Age Three

Last January, when the war against Iraq was started, I was in Mexico writing a novel about a woman who is genitally mutilated in a ritual of female circumcision that her society imposes on all females. Genital mutilation is a mental and physical health hazard that directly affects some one hundred million women and girls worldwide, alive today, to whom it has been done. Because of increased risk of trauma during delivery, it affects the children to whom they give birth. Indirectly, because of its linkage to the spread of AIDS, especially among women and children, it affects the health and well-being of everyone on the planet.

With no television or radio, and no real eagerness to see or hear arrogant Western males discussing their military prowess, their delight in their own "cleanhanded" destructiveness, I relied on a friend's phone calls to his son in San Francisco to keep me informed. His son told us about the huge resistance to the war in San Francisco, which made me love the city even more than I did already, and informed us too that he had been one of those demonstrators so outraged that they'd closed down the Bay Bridge.

What to do? Go home and join the demonstrations, or continue to write about the fact that little girls' bodies are daily "bombed" by dull knives, rusty tin can tops and scissors, shards of unwashed glass—and that this is done to them not by a foreign power but by their own parents? I decided to stay put. To continue this story about genital mutilation, aka "female circumcision," which I believe is vital for the world to hear. But of course I could not forget the war being waged against the earth and the people of Iraq.

Because I was thinking so hard about the suffering of little girls, while grieving over the frightened people trying to flee our government's bombs, my unconscious, in trying to help me balance my thoughts, did a quite wonderful thing. It gave me a substitute for Saddam Hussein, the "demon" on whom the United States military's bombs were falling. Her name was *Sadie* Hussein, and she was three years old. So, as the bombs were falling, I thought about Sadie Hussein, with her bright dark eyes and chubby cheeks, her shiny black curls and her dainty pink dress, and I put my arms around her. I could not, however, save her.

As it turned out, this was the truth. Saddam Hussein still reigns, at least as secure in his power over the Iraqis, according to some media sources, as George Bush is over North Americans. It is Sadie Hussein who is being destroyed, and who, along with nine hundred thousand other Iraqi children under the age of five, is dying of cholera, malnutrition, infection, and diarrhea. Since the war, fifty thousand such children have died. It is Sadie Hussein who starves daily on less than half her body's nutritional needs, while Saddam Hussein actually appears to have gained weight.

This is the story of why I am here today. I am here because I pay taxes. More money in taxes in one year than my sharecropping parents, descendants of enslaved Africans and Indians, earned in a lifetime. My taxes helped pay for Sadie Hussein's suffering and death. The grief I feel about this will accompany me to my grave. I believe war is a weapon of persons without personal power, that is to say, the power to reason, the power to persuade, from a position of morality and integrity; and that to go to war with any enemy who is weaker than you is to admit you possess no resources within yourself to bring to bear on your own fate. I will think of George Bush vomiting once into the lap of the Japanese prime minister and will immediately see hundreds of thousands of Iraqi children, cold, hungry, dying of fever, dysentery, typhoid, and every other sickness, vomiting endlessly into the laps of their mothers—who are also emaciated, starving, terrorized, and so illiterate they are unable to read Saddam Hussein's name, no matter how large he writes it.

The slaughter of Iraqis and the destruction of so much of the earth deeply disturbed the world. Many of us could not ignore the pain in our hearts when we heard various United States government rumblings of: Cuba is next.

It is difficult to think of Cuba without also thinking of Fidel Castro. In fact, I cannot entirely do it, for I do not think of him at all as the demon he has been set up to be over the past thirty-odd years. Whereas I recognize Saddam Hussein as a victim of gross child abuse who grew up to abuse and victimize his people in the same way he was terrorized and tortured as a child, I recognize in Fidel Castro the Jesuit scholar and social-activist lawyer; a lover of children and a defender of the weak and the oppressed; a secular "priest" who finally picked up the gun. Though an atheist, he is nevertheless a person of immense spiritual power, and it is true to say, I believe, that the Cuban Revolution, all these years, has been fueled by his revolutionary spirit. In his love of the most humble of the Cuban people, and of the Cuban spirit per se, he is not unlike the Dalai Lama, whose devotion to Tibet and Tibetan culture is absolute.

Saddam Hussein, a convenient villain for the West because he is obviously out of balance psychologically, tortures and bombs his own population. Though an attempt is frequently made in the media to equate Hussein and Fidel, and this is easy, visually, because they are both "dark" and wear uniforms, I feel we must be vigilant about noting differences, and affirming them. Just for our own clarity and human integrity.

However, what is more important is that we remember that wars—whether waged through military strikes, as against Iraq, or through trade embargoes and blockades, as in the case of Cuba— are fought not against leaders only but against the people, who may or may not even like the leader. And that children are the most devastated victims.

Thirteen years ago I went to Cuba, and the radiant health, intelligence, generosity, and joyousness of the people made it a sacred place for me. Ironically, in a place where there was very little Church, I felt the most God.

Since I was born into the poorest, least powerful, most despised population of the United States and was spoken to as if I were a dog when I asked to use a library or eat in a restaurant, the revelation that people of color, who make up between 40 and 60 percent of Cuba's population, and women, who make up half, can share in all the fruits of their labors was a major gift Cuba gave to me—a major encouragement to struggle for equality and justice, and one I shall never forget.

I refuse to be responsible for the suffering and death of hundreds or thousands of Fidelitos and Fidelitas. My ego is not stroked by the thought of sick and hungry Cuban children throwing up in their tired, scared, ill mothers' arms. What gives me pleasure is the thought that all children everywhere can be safe from deliberate brutality and cruelty, deliberate enslavement, ignorance, and genocide.

Rather than envying—as I think the United States government does—and therefore despising Cuba for its dedication to the health of its citizens and its elevation of people of color, women, and the poor, I believe it has important lessons to teach our gadget-rich but spiritually bankrupt country: that the earth on which we live is the body of God. All people and living things are the body and soul of God. And that we serve God not by making the earth and its people suffer but by making the earth and its people whole. This is why I have always believed Fidel Castro is really a priest. We can look at the sound teeth, shining eyes, straight limbs, and strong minds of the Cuban people today and know that thirty-odd years ago these same people would have been null and void. After thirty-odd years of racism, sexism, poverty, assassinations, and despair in the United States, great numbers of my own generation—because of homelessness, joblessness, drugs—are certainly null and void.

I am far from blind to Cuba's imperfections. There are days when I think: How noble, how graceful, it would be if Fidel Castro would simply retire. I think: Doesn't he have grandchildren to snuggle and jiggle on his knee before he dies? I also think this about George Bush and all the rest of the rich white male dictatorship we in North America suffer under. And have suffered under since the arrival of these men five hundred years ago. I am also highly skeptical of a revolution that has not produced younger men and women to lead it. But one thing is clear: Whatever its imperfections, in Cuba the poor have not been held in contempt; they have been empowered. Which is different from being made wealthy in a capitalist sense, and more lasting. A healthy body, a well-trained mind, a sense of solidarity with one's people, these are harder to lose than a million dollars, and offer more security. This empowerment of the poor—literacy, good health, adequate housing, freedom from ignorance—is the work of everyone of conscience in the coming century. Cuba has led the way and is an object lesson to us. For, if the poor are not empowered—by any means at their disposal—they will continue to be devoured by the rich. Just as women, if not empowered, will continue to be the slaves of men.

I have heard that rich Cubans in Miami (whose old money was no doubt made off the backs of slaves and the vulvas of women), and others who see Cuba as real estate, intend to buy Cuba, as if it were still the North American–owned plantation it was before the revolution. This is obscene. What has been paid for in blood, tears, and backbreaking work by the people of Cuba cannot be bought, especially not by rich white Cubans in Miami, or by those North American profiteers who raped Cuba shamelessly over hundreds of years and who, if they returned to that land today, would hardly recognize it. Certainly it would surprise them not to encounter any of their former slaves, serfs, drug addicts, and prostitutes— though prostitution has, tragically, returned, as Cuba's economic situation has worsened and disproportionate emphasis has been placed on tourism.

What can I tell you? Cubans always speak of defending the revolution. I speak of defending ourselves from the grief and heartbreak of being accomplices to evil acts done in our name and with our hard-earned cash. I speak of defending our right not to be murderers. If I would rather die myself than run over a child in the street, how can I possibly accept squashing a million children from forty-five thousand feet, as in Iraq? And to celebrate such a feat, I assure you, is quite impossible. To see the anti-abortion forces, including Bush, rage against poor and scared women, some of them homeless, who refuse to give life to children they cannot support, while not even planting symbolic crosses for the actual children bombed to death in Iraq, is to witness cynicism in its most unconscionable form. I speak of defending our right to praise and uphold what is good about any other people's way of life, even as we recognize and criticize what is bad. To Cuba I would say, Your poets are the heartbeat of the revolution, because that is what, by definition, poets are. If you force them to eat their words, it is the revolution that will suffer indigestion and massive heart attack.* Bread is not everything, after all, as women have always stressed; there must be roses too. And the roses of any revolution are the uncertainties one dares to share.

I speak of defending the Earth, our Mother God. I speak of defending and loving the Earth's children: All of Us.

---

* This refers to an article I read about a Cuban poet who wrote poems against the Cuban government. Neighbors allegedly forced the poet to eat the poems.

Suffice it to say that at one point we had three times more doctors working for free in the Third World than did the World Health Organization; and we didn't have a lot of resources either, only minimum resources. We only had the honor of our health workers, with their internationalist calling. How many lives have they saved? And I wonder, is it fair to blockade a country that has done this?

More than 26,000 Cuban teachers have served abroad. How many hundreds of thousands of children have we educated with our teachers in foreign countries? And we haven't only sent primary and secondary school teachers, but university professors. We have founded medical schools in diverse countries of the world. Is it fair to blockade a country that has done all this, and still does it to a certain degree?

Half a million Cubans have completed internationalist missions of different types, half a million Cubans! I ask if any other small country, and even medium or big countries, has had this record.

The Africans have been very generous, very noble, and have wanted to recall here Cuba's solidarity and aid in the war against colonialism, the war against foreign aggression, the war against apartheid and racism.

As I said here, our soldiers were fighting in southern Angola — 40,000 men! They were fighting alongside the Angolan troops, who acted and fought heroically. There were Cubans in southern Angola facing up to the South Africans after the battle of Cuito Cuanavale, and when our counteroffensive was launched in southwest Angola these men and women were exposed to the possibility of nuclear warfare. We knew it, and the distribution of forces in that offensive took into account the possibility that the enemy could use nuclear weapons.

—FIDEL CASTRO
*World Solidarity Conference
Havana, Cuba
November 25, 1994*

Hugging Fidel

WHAT IF THERE'S A TORTURE CHAMBER UNDERNEATH THE PALACIO DE LA REVOLUCIÓN?

There are moments that we will remember always. We know this as they are happening. There is a subtle light around them. A feeling of a circle being closed. They have a sound that is distinct but indescribable, as they feed something old and weary, something hungry in the soul. There is an urge to laugh, though the joy is heavy with sorrow. They are moments, often, with a long history of longing behind them, of shared suffering and losses. Moments that have, as well, memories of happiness, of triumph over evil, of solidarity with irrepressible warriors and a temporary distance from defeat.

One such moment for me was hugging Fidel Castro Ruz the second time I was in Cuba, in 1992. It was not a planned hug. In fact, on the way to the Palacio de la Revolución in Havana, in a clean but old North American bus, I had no idea what might happen. I had spent the previous evening with a stunningly beautiful black woman who had escaped from prison in the United States and been a guest of the Cuban people for nearly two decades. She had been charged with killing a highway patrolman, a charge she denied, claiming that her real crime had been to be part of a black revolutionary group in the late Sixties, targeted for destruction by the F.B.I.; her comrades, in the confrontation with the patrol, deserted her. I was so intensely glad to find her alive—speaking Spanish and driving a tiny, battered car ("But how do you get gasoline?" I asked. "By any means necessary," she replied, grinning)—that by the time I left her small, colorfully decorated house, I felt emotionally worn out.

In the morning I had been helping to deliver medicines to a children's hospital and talking to doctors, nurses, gravely ill children, and their mothers. I didn't know if I could bear any more emotion. I had been glad that a visit with Fidel seemed out of the question, until it was unexpectedly announced after dinner, and suddenly everyone was ready to go. In the United States, Fidel Castro has been demonized by the press, castigated by presidents and others in government for over thirty years. Suppose, after years of admiring him from afar, I discovered that, up close, I didn't like him either.

I wouldn't be able to hide it.

As the bus carried us through the quiet streets of Havana, where, because of the gas shortage, few cars were in evidence, I meditated on my long relationship to the Cuban people, on the Cuban Revolution, on the lives of men and women who are as precious to me as Sojourner Truth, John Brown, Malcolm X or Martin Luther King, Jr., Harriet Tubman or Jesse Jackson, and on my long-term feelings of closeness to the least dashing of the revolutionaries who stormed the Moncada barracks in 1953, thereby beginning the Cuban Revolution—the bearded and loquacious lawyer Fidel Castro Ruz. I thought of Camilio Cienfuego, of Che Guevara, of Celia Sanchez, of Haydée Santamaria and her brother Abel Santamaria, all dead, having given their lives in the fight to give the Cuban people a change, and a chance at life. I had been deeply moved and inspired by all of them. The Cuban Revolution was my generation's Chiapas.

In 1959, when Fidel came to power, I was sixteen and living in the brutally racist, completely segregated state of Georgia. Fascism was a way of life, so entrenched there seemed no other possibility. I could neither eat at a public restaurant nor use a public library or rest room without the certainty of being arrested by a white male agent of the state who would undoubtedly physically or verbally abuse me. For a long time I could not even identify with the tiny bits of news coming from the Cuban people's struggle, because the faces we saw—Fidel and his comrades living as guerrillas in the jungles of the Sierra Maestra or rolling triumphantly through the streets of Havana—were white.

What if you discover a Cuban gulag? a friend had joked as I packed for the trip. What if there's a torture chamber underneath the Palacio de la Revolución? What about the skeletons that are probably in Fidel's closet? What about the concentration camps where they keep gay people with AIDS? Having read the newspapers for several years, she thought about Cuba this way. Having visited once and kept in touch through friends and books and organizations that monitored the island regularly, I had different expectations. When I thought of Cuba I thought of a health care system that was one of the best in the world. Of how well educated Cubans are. Of their zest for life and their love of music, reading, dance, and talk. I thought of a place that welcomed me. A place, unlike the Georgia, U.S.A., of my birth, where I did not feel afraid. Now, because of the collapse of the Soviet Union and the ever-tightening United States embargo, I worried that every gain in health care, literacy, and housing would be wiped out. That Cuba might be returned to its former poverty under the dictatorship of Fulgencio Batista, a former overseer of Cuba, as a plantation for U.S. interests.

I identified with Fidel because he was fighting the same greedy men we were also fighting, and as a student I thought often of him and of Che Guevara, and of their guerrilla fighting down from the Sierra Maestra and into revolutionary power in Havana. As we were beaten, battered by firehoses, thrown into jail for demanding the right to eat and sleep in public establishments, and also the more important right to vote, the Cuban Revolution gave me hope. These were men and women who had not backed down, though faced with the cruelest repression. They had a dream of equality and justice, of bread and roses, of exemplary high schools and world-class hospitals; they stated as early goals that they intended to teach every Cuban to read and to produce enough doctors to export them to every poor third-world country on earth. How could anyone resist this revolution? Especially as the Cubans, with small resources but plenty of courage and help from wherever they could get it, set out to make their dream come true.

The day before, I had gone to visit one of the "concentration camps for gays with AIDS." I was a big hit there, much to my surprise. Everyone had read *The Color Purple* or seen the movie; everyone was a huge Steven Spielberg fan. Several had read *The Temple of My Familiar* in translation. The moment I got off the bus and was introduced, two men linked arms with me and walked me away from my group. When we arrived at their cottage they asked if I'd brought books with me. I had. They wanted to know if I would accept handmade items they wished to give me as gifts. I did. They wanted to know if, in the United States, there was any new drug, newer than AZT, that might save their lives. I had no idea. This information was of utmost importance to them; when I said I didn't know, they looked stricken. We chatted about the scarcity of condoms on the island and how the U.S. embargo prevented their import. Cuba has a very low rate of HIV infection, I was told, largely because of its implementation of a plan to isolate those with AIDS from the rest of the population.

Their simple cottages were scattered over many acres and resembled a Southern college campus. They explained that they were bored, but otherwise felt well cared for. While quarantined they were being taught how not to infect their partners and others sexually, and would soon be able to travel home for weekend vis-

its. Many couples, both gay and heterosexual, shared small apart-
ments. These spaces were neat, furnished simply, with lots of plants,
and quiet. During the rest of the visit we saw where everyone
worked: shops in which patients create printed cloth, leather
goods, masks and figurines of papier-mâché.

The bus stops near a huge statue of Lenin, I think, but on closer
inspection it is José Martí, the beloved inspiration of Cuban resistance, who, in white marble, looks remarkably like his Russian
counterpart. Excited, we climb the steps of the Palacio de la Revolución. In the green room we wait. I am with a delegation that
includes workers, teachers, activists, and a couple of ophthalmologists. Also Dennis Banks of the American Indian Movement and
former United States attorney general Ramsey Clark. Within minutes Fidel appears, along with his interpreter. She is dressed in a
brown skirt and a deep rose blouse. Fidel is wearing silken green
fatigues, more elegant up close than on television, and she looks
like a flower at his side. Two aides wearing guayaberas trail behind.
Fidel is sixty-six years old. Though his beard is gray, he looks as
handsome now as when he was young. I've read somewhere that
he does a lot of underwater fishing, and it shows; he seems in very
good shape. I feel I've been aware of him all my conscious life. For
I did not really awaken until I heard the call to resist oppression
that he and Martin Luther King, Jr., seemed to utter at the same
moment. He is really tall. Slowly he moves around the room to
greet each person. When he gets to me, he mentions having seen
me on television the night before, when I had talked about my sadness at witnessing the worry and anxiety on the faces of Cubans
agonizing over the shortage of food. He smiles as he takes my
hand. They didn't kill you; I'm so glad, I think, looking up at him
and remembering other revolutionaries the C.I.A. did manage to
assassinate.
    His daughter, who came to the United States a few months after
my visit, has called him a "dinosaur," a "relic" from another time.

He did bring into the room with him that evening something of the past; the green uniform seemed part of a commitment to fight on that not everyone cared to remember. I have always felt that Fidel chose to be a revolutionary as a monk chooses to be a priest; it is a calling to which he is pledged. The uniform is his cassock. He is a religious person whose god is revolution. His way of "giving to the poor." Looking at his tall, straight back and his almost courtly grace, I mused, Robin Hood also wore green his whole merry life.

But Fidel is not merry, as we sit later around a large table listening to him. He is speaking urgently, angrily, with a dark look on his face. He looks distinctly demonic. At any moment I expect him to start tearing at his hair. I immediately think of his friend Gabriel García Márquez, and of his depiction of lugubrious Latin American generals in his novels, all mad with egotism and loneliness. Fidel is talking and talking and glaring at the two ophthalmologists, one of them a petite blond woman, the other a slender Japanese-American man. They are both from New York. For some reason the interpreter is late starting to translate. When she does, we learn what Fidel is raging about: an epidemic of blindness that is sweeping the island and affecting mainly young men.* The ophthalmologists are mentioning victims they have seen and suggesting possible reasons for the disease. Fidel has apparently stayed up nights researching the problem and is now running through the extensive information he knows. He also tells us what he fears: that the epidemic might be the result of chemical warfare introduced by the United States. It has been a long time since I've seen anyone so agitated, so troubled. Or so completely unconcerned about how upset he appears. It is not unlike being in the presence of a distraught parent, or of a betrayed child.

By the time he begins talking with Dennis Banks, Fidel is more calm; his tone is sardonic. He knows a lot about the history of Indi-

---

* Optic neuropathy. At the time of my visit it had affected some forty thousand people.

ans in the United States, as well as those elsewhere in the Americas. He says Europe has not stopped raping the New World and is currently taking out even more gold than during colonial times. "We are all Indians now," he says, after listening intently to Dennis. He is very present while each of us speaks, and he asks penetrating, thoughtful questions. He and Ramsey Clark seem to be on very friendly terms. I marvel at this: Clark, from Texas, once the attorney general of the United States, today makes it his business to lobby for the right of the Cuban people to exist as they choose. He tells Fidel how privileged we all feel to be bringing medicine to a country that has done so much to heal others. He is wonderful and speaks passionately from the heart. He looks like such a typical Yankee that the contradiction brings tears to my eyes.

My statement about the prevalence of female genital mutilation in Africa and elsewhere startles Fidel; I have the impression he really feels he knows something about just about everything and is amazed that this information escaped him. He seems genuinely disturbed. When I mention how odd it seems to me that so many Cuban doctors have worked in Africa and never, apparently, mentioned this practice to anyone in Cuba, he seems irritated. "They may have known of this," he says. "I just didn't know."

But when I push a stack of my books across the table to him, he brightens. "*The Color Purple* in Spanish," he exclaims. "Just what I've wanted!" He opens *The Temple of My Familiar* (in Spanish, *El Templo de Mis Amigos*) and begins to read it! He mutters how sick he is of reading government reports and how much he enjoys reading novels. As a writer of novels, I am thrilled.

After an hour or so of conversation, and plenty of monologue, we are invited into the large reception hall of the Palacio de la Revolución. It is a delightful space, bare except for giant ferns, transferred from the Sierra Maestra, that seem to grow out of the walls. It is said that this hall was designed by Fidel's former soulmate and *compañera,* Celia Sanchez, who died some years ago of cancer. Fidel offers us tidbits of chicken and tasty rum drinks called *mojitos,* apologizing for the limited supply and lack of variety. He continues to talk, answering questions energetically and thoroughly, the members of our delegation in a tight cluster around him. He enjoys talking. Or maybe it's compulsive. There are many funny stories of his ability to go on and on, sometimes through the night. Looking at and listening to Fidel, I think how monologists must always seem dictatorial, simply because they are always speaking.

I think about an interview I gave to a reporter from a radio station in Australia. He'd asked me why I participated in activity aimed at lifting the U.S. embargo against Cuba. I said I'd done it out of respect and admiration for the Cuban people, who had done me only good, never harm. And because I vote and pay taxes, I added, and the ability to express my disagreement with government policy is part of what it means to be an American citizen. He began to rant, literally, about how Fidel Castro was a dictator, and did my activity mean I condoned dictatorship? I was so taken aback by his vehemence I could only say what I basically feel: That Fidel Castro has tried to improve the condition of poor people in his country and has, in fact, done so. That to blame him alone for Cuba's troubles is simplistic and unfair. A more pertinent inquiry might be why the United States, while refusing to trade with Cuba and preventing other countries from doing so—because Cuba is not a "free society"—trades with, for instance, Nigeria, Indonesia, and China, countries with the most abominable human rights records. Does this mean the United States condones mass murder, kidnapping, assassination, imprisonment for political belief, forced marriage, slavery, and in the case of China's occupation of Tibet, genocide?

What I thought after the interview was something else. I was annoyed to think that a white Australian man actually believes he lives in something other than a dictatorship. Or that people anywhere believe they actually have democracy. What most people live under in the West is a white male dictatorship, although the particular white male leader is periodically changed; almost everywhere the dictatorship is male. Could anyone really think Native Americans, Australian aboriginal people, the Maori of New

Zealand, or black people in the United States believe we live in anything other than a dictatorship? A regime put in place by white men, for white men, who dictate everything most people eat, think, and wear? Where even sexual fantasies and spiritual yearnings are controlled by media that are owned, almost entirely, by men who are rich and white? And what about women, the majority of humans on the planet? If there were democracy, we'd represent, politically speaking, half the power of the world. What about children, who have no say in their government at all? It is, of course, deepest cynicism to boast of democracy after having slain and enslaved the majority of the nonwhite people encountered or "found."*

I do think Fidel should retire. But I don't think so for the same reasons advanced by Bush and Clinton and Dole, who seem to feel they are somehow better leaders than he is, and who exhibit a truly sickening ability to cast the first stone. I read in the paper one day that Fidel was finally visiting his father's village in Spain, and that while there he'd mentioned being "the slave of the revolution." In this statement I felt his weariness. For over three decades he has defied the mightiest country on earth. He has watched his best friends and allies shrivel and fall. He has survived numerous assassination attempts by the C.I.A. Only Nelson Mandela is perhaps his equal in terms of determination, self-sacrifice, and loss. There is a moving photograph of Mandela and Castro embracing when, after his almost thirty years in prison, Mandela went to Cuba to personally thank Fidel and the Cuban people for helping to turn back South Africa's armies in the Front Line states, thereby playing a major role in the liberation of South Africa.

Though his father was a wealthy landowner during Fidel's childhood, he had left Spain poor, and in Cuba had sold homemade lemonade from a cart. His mother, about whom one hears

---

* For anyone who still believes the United States is a democracy and not a white male corporate dictatorship, I recommend the book *Partners in Power: The Clintons' America,* by Roger Morris.

little, except that she was originally his father's cook and was very religious and that Fidel adored her, probably instilled in her son a love of and belief in the poor he has never forgotten. I believe Fidel was deeply inspired by these two. They named him "Faithful," after his godfather. It is a lot to live up to.

I do not believe in male-only leadership anywhere in the world, including Cuba. I think the woman at Fidel's side should be his co-president, not his interpreter. Nor do I wish to imitate Frida Kahlo, one of whose last paintings was of "Uncle" Joe Stalin, whose attempts to improve the lives of Russians she respected and about whose gulags and genocidal policies she knew nothing. There is no way of knowing yet what skeletons, if any, are gleaming in Fidel's closet. Or if they are worse than Clinton's, Kennedy's, Gingrich's, or Dole's. For years the United States media have been pulling out bones that almost never, once you actually go to Cuba and talk to Cubans, connect, except grotesquely, to the reality of life there and the dreams and aspirations of the people. As an outsider I have nothing to go on but the universal evidence of healthy bodies, sound teeth, and self-possessed spirits so lacking in many other third-world countries; the excellence Cubans exhibit in so many areas, including medicine, education, and sports. Even the Cuban boat people, escaping from the devastation and hunger of their island, were remarkable for their fitness, their ingenuity in constructing their boats, and often for their ability to speak more than one language.

While Fidel is talking, talking, I think about those ten pounds we have been told every Cuban has lost because of a shortage of food. I had noticed the neatness and sheen of his uniform, and Fidel's apparent good health; now I take a closer look. The worst thing in the world, I think, would be to see a fat leader in the land of the lean. But even without looking hard, or particularly noting the slackness of his belt, which even droops a bit on one side, I can see Fidel is considerably thinner than he was when he bought his uniform. I think of reports of him, as a younger man, cutting sugar cane side by side with other Cubans, women and men, bringing in the crucial sugar harvest. I've often asked myself how a strong, well-fed, militarily secure nation like the United States could demean itself by torturing a small country like Cuba, just because its leader refuses to knuckle under. Perhaps the answer is that no matter how crazy and out of touch Fidel is made to appear in the United States media, a huge threat to North America's ego, he nonetheless never seems separate from the Cuban people.

It amuses me that he can talk so long and that he expects his audience to stand just as long as he does. I'm tired by now and can't. Besides, all I want to ask him about is his mother. I go over to the side of the room and sit down. I am soon joined by another member of our group. When speaking, I have read, Fidel must have every ear, and sure enough, he notices and is distracted by our absence; several times he glances over at us. We smile but stay where we are. He seems so human. I feel very tender toward him. I have the feeling he is a brother I miraculously have; it has been decades since I thought of him as white. It would break my heart if his skeletons are really bad. What are the chances, I wonder, that they're not? And how many times has my heart already been broken? And is it by now only more flexible, or is it more cracked? Not to mention that I don't believe, anymore, in leaders. Nor am I crazy about uniforms. The courage to stand with the poor I like. I drift back over. He is obviously glad that we have returned. He towers over us, like the last giant redwood in a clear-cut forest, so alive, so green, still, this man who inspired me to fight for my young life. I know I could never thank him enough for the shelter of his example, no matter what. Can I give you a hug? I ask, and it seems I hold many long, dark nights in my arms, nights of despair when I cried for Malcolm, for Martin, for Abel, for Che. For Rosa Parks and Fannie Lou. For my poor sharecropping parents, who never had anyone to fight for them, and for myself, who have fought long and hard, only to see today, in our drug-and-crime-and-poverty-infested "democracy," the near ruin of my people. Fidel's nights, I am sure, have been just as dark and long. His mornings just as bereft. Still, now, we are beaming. Impulsively kissing the top of my head, he returns my embrace warmly, like a man who understands what he is holding, like a man who has fought all his life for just such a time.

As we leave the room, I tell him what I have come to tell him. Private words I have wanted to say to him for thirty years. He responds promptly with a gracefulness that touches my heart. I know we will never meet again. But, as the ancient Native Americans chanted, *It is finished in beauty.* Whatever my government does, I will always act as friend and neighbor to the Cuban people. I will never make war on this man.

POSTSCRIPT: In less than two years I was to see Fidel again. In the spring of 1994 I received a fax from Leslie Cagan of the United States and Cuba Medical Project, asking if I would lead a delegation of women who would deliver five million dollars' worth of antibiotics to Cuba. I said yes, with joy. I called Pratibha Parmar and Angela Davis and asked them to join me. Our all-woman delegation included Davis and Parmar, Cagan and Rachel Cohen of the United States and Cuba Medical Project, and Kathy Engle of Madre, an organization that lends support to women and children in beleaguered countries around the world, of which I am also a member.

After delivering the antibiotics, donated by North American pharmaceutical firms, to the Cuban Red Cross, we were invited to visit the Palacio de la Revolución to talk with Fidel. Like so many Cubans, Fidel was obviously delighted to see Angela Davis again, and they reminisced about their friendship of twenty-odd years earlier, when Angela, recently released from prison in the United States, was in Cuba, secluded in the mountains, writing her autobiography.

He was fascinated by her long, copper-colored dreadlocks (when she was in Cuba before, she'd had an enormous Afro), and I was amused to see him surreptitiously examining a lock with his fingers when they embraced and he thought no one was looking.

This inquisitiveness, curiosity about another's reality, endeared him to me on this visit, as did his apparent pleasure in being called upon by so many wild women. The six of us had been swimming in a river earlier in the afternoon and had not expected to visit the president of the country directly after, or at all. So there we were. Angela in shorts and sneakers, me in damp and very baggy jeans, Rachel in a mini-dress that barely covered particulars. Everybody's hair every which way. Beaming back at this revolutionary old man who doesn't remind any of us of Stalin, and who thanked us for the medicine we brought to his country and said it made him so happy to see us.

*Robert Allen and Alice Walker protesting the U.S. government's
shipment of weapons to Central America. Concord Naval Weapons
Station, Concord, California, June 12, 1987. My T-shirt says:
"Remember Port Chicago," where over three hundred enlisted men,
mainly black, were blown to bits when the bombs they were loading
onto a ship during World War II blew up.
Port Chicago was renamed Concord.*

PHOTO BY BELVIE ROOKS

A Letter to President Clinton

President Bill Clinton
The White House
Washington, D.C.
March 13, 1996

Dear President Clinton:

Thank you very much for the invitation to visit the White House while I was in Washington in January. I am sorry circumstances made it impossible for us to meet. I was looking forward to experiencing the symbolic seat of North American government in a new way. In the past, I have only picketed the White House, and as a student walking up and down the street outside it, I used to wonder what might be inside. It seemed to be made of cardboard, and appeared empty and oppressive, remote from the concerns of a few black students—and their courageous white teacher*—from the Deep South.

The first protest I joined that picketed the White House was a Hands Off Cuba rally in 1962. I was eighteen. It was very cold—snow and sleet everywhere. Our hands and feet and heads were

---

* Radical historian Staughton Lynd, who was also valiantly active in opposing the Vietnam War.

freezing as we trudged in circles, shouting slogans to keep our minds off our misery and to encourage each other. Amazingly, someone from the president's office sent hot coffee out to us. This compassionate gesture humanized the president and the White House for me, and made it possible for me to feel a connection that I would not otherwise have felt. When President Kennedy was assassinated, and my whole school wept, it was of those warming sips of coffee that I thought.

I love Cuba and its people, including Fidel. The bill you have signed to further tighten the blockade hurts me deeply. I travel to Cuba whenever I can, to take medicine and the small, perhaps insignificant, comfort of my presence, to those whose courage and tenderness have inspired me practically my entire life.

I have seen how the embargo hurts everyone in Cuba, but especially Cuban children, infants in particular. I spend some nights in utter sleeplessness worrying about them. Someone has said that when you give birth to a child—and perhaps I read this in Hillary's book, which I recently bought—you are really making a commitment to the agony of having your heart walking around outside your body. That is how I feel about Cuba; I am quite unable to think of it as separate from myself. I have taken seriously the beliefs and values I learned from my Georgia parents, the most sincere and humble Christians I have ever known: Do unto others . . . Love thy neighbor . . . All of it. I feel the suffering of each child in Cuba as if it were my own.

This bill you have signed is wrong.* Even if you despise Fidel and even if the Cubans should not have shot down the planes violating their airspace.† (Did you, by the way, see Oliver Stone's *Earth*

---

* The Helms-Burton bill would make it possible for complainants to sue foreign companies and exclude their executives from U.S. soil if these entities profit in any way from property that was seized during the Cuban Revolution of 1959 and whose former owners are now U.S. citizens.

† On February 24, 1996, the Cuban air force shot down two Brothers to the Rescue planes which, it claimed, had repeatedly violated Cuban airspace.

and Sky, about the U.S. bombing and general destruction of Vietnam? Over years and years. *There* was a major case of violating airspace!) The bill is wrong, the embargo is wrong, because it punishes people, some of them unborn, for being who they are. Cubans cannot help being who they are. Given their long struggle for freedom, particularly from Spain and the United States, they cannot help taking understandable pride in who they are. They have chosen a way of life different from ours, and I must say, from my limited exposure to that different way of life, it has brought them, fundamentally, a deep inner certainty about the meaning of existence (to develop oneself and to help others) and an equally deep psychic peace. One endearing quality I've found in the Cubans I have met is that they can listen with as much heart as they speak.

I believe you and Fidel must speak to each other. Face-to-face. He is not the monster he has been portrayed as being; and in all the study you have done of Cuba, surely it is apparent to you that he has reason for being the leader he is. Nor am I saying he is without flaw. We are all substantially flawed, wounded, angry, hurt, here on Earth. But this human condition, so painful to us, and in some ways shameful—because we feel we are weak when the reality of ourselves is exposed—is made much more bearable when it is shared, face-to-face, in words that have expressive human eyes behind them. Beyond any other reason for talking with Fidel, I think you would enjoy it.

In 1962 I also went to Russia. I was determined to impress upon all the Russians I met that I was not their enemy, and that I opposed the idea my government had at that time of possibly killing all of them. I have never regretted offering smiles to the children of Russia, instead of agreeing with a paranoid government to throw bombs.

The world, I believe, is easier to change than we think. And harder. Because the change begins with each one of us saying to ourselves, and meaning it: *I will not harm anyone or anything in this moment.* Until, like recovering alcoholics, we can look back on an hour, a day, a week, a year, of comparative harmlessness.

Is Jesse Helms, who speaks of Cuban liberty as he urges our country to harm Cuba's citizens, the same Jesse Helms who caused my grandparents, my parents, and my own generation profound suffering as we struggled against our enslavement under racist laws in the South? And can it be that you have joined your name to his, in signing this bill? Although this is fact, it still strikes me as unbelievable. Inconceivable. I cannot think his is a name you will rejoice in later years to have associated with your own. I regret this action, sincerely, for your sake.

The country has lost its way, such as it was. Primarily because it is now understood by all that resources and space itself are limited, and the days of infinite expansion and exploitation, sometimes referred to as "growth," are over. Greed has been a primary motivating factor from the beginning. And so the dream of the revengeful and the greedy is to retake Cuba, never mind the cries of children who can no longer have milk to drink, or of adults whose ration card permits them one egg a week. Would you want Chelsea to have no milk, to have one egg a week? You are a large man, how would you yourself survive?

My heart goes out to you—I voted for you for president, even though I personally want compassionate feminine leadership in the world, at least for the next hundred years or so: uncompassionate woman-hating and child-forgetful masculine leadership has pretty much destroyed us—because I know the same forces that have demonized Fidel for so long are after you and especially Hillary. I wonder if you can see this? Or if you really feel secure and confident of the future, standing shoulder to shoulder with the Republicans and with Helms?

Sometimes, when I don't know what to do, I imagine a little child standing beside my desk, or sometimes a small baby, kicking, *on* my desk. There are Cuban children—as dear as any on earth, as dear as Chelsea, or my daughter, Rebecca—standing beside your desk all the time now. How could this not be so? They are standing beside the desks of those in Congress, in the Senate. They are standing in our grossly overstuffed supermarkets and spying on us in Weight Watchers. One cannot justify starving them to death because their leader is a person of whom some people, themselves imperfect, human, disapprove.

America at the moment is like a badly wounded parent, the aging, spent, and scared offspring of all the dysfunctional families of the multitudes of tribes who settled here. It is the medicine of compassionate understanding that must be administered now, immediately, on a daily basis, indiscriminately. Not the poison of old patterns of punishment and despair. *Harmlessness now!* must be our peace cry.

I often disagree with you—your treatment of black women, of Lani Guinier and the wonderful Joycelyn Elders in particular, has caused me to feel a regrettable distance. Still, I care about you, Hillary, and Chelsea and wish you only good. I certainly would not deprive you of food in protest of anything you have done!

Similarly, I will always love and respect the Cuban people, and help them whenever I can. Their way of caring for all humanity has made them my family. Whenever you hurt them, or help them, please think of me.

Sincerely,
Alice Walker

My Mother's Blue Bowl

Visitors to my house are often served food—soup, potatoes, rice—in a large blue stoneware bowl, noticeably chipped at the rim. It is perhaps the most precious thing I own. It was given to me by my mother in her last healthy days. The days before a massive stroke laid her low and left her almost speechless. Those days when to visit her was to be drawn into a serene cocoon of memories and present-day musings and to rest there, in temporary retreat from the rest of the world, as if still an infant, nodding and secure at her breast.

For much of her life my mother longed, passionately longed, for a decent house. One with a yard that did not have to be cleared with an ax. One with a roof that kept out the rain. One with floors that you could not fall through. She longed for a beautiful house of wood or stone. Or of red brick, like the houses her many sisters and their husbands had. When I was thirteen she found such a house. Green-shuttered, white-walled. Breezy. With a lawn and a hedge and giant pecan trees. A porch swing. There her gardens flourished in spite of the shade, as did her youngest daughter, for whom she sacrificed her life doing hard labor in someone else's house, in order to afford peace and prettiness for her child, to whose grateful embrace she returned each night.

But, curiously, the minute I left home, at seventeen, to attend college, she abandoned the dream house and moved into the projects. Into a small, tight apartment of few breezes, in which I was never to feel comfortable, but that she declared suited her "to a T." I took solace in the fact that it was at least hugged by spacious lawn on one side, and by forest, out the back door, and that its isolated position at the end of the street meant she would have a measure of privacy.

Her move into the projects—the best housing poor black people in the South ever had, she would occasionally declare, even as my father struggled to adjust to the cramped rooms and hard, unforgiving qualities of brick—was, I now understand, a step in the direction of divestiture, lightening her load, permitting her worldly possessions to dwindle in significance and, well before she herself would turn to spirit, roll away from her.

She owned little, in fact. A bed, a dresser, some chairs. A set of living-room furniture. A set of kitchen furniture. A bed and wardrobe (given to her years before, when I was a teenager, by one of her more prosperous sisters). Her flowers: everywhere, inside the house and outside. Planted in anything she managed to get her green hands on, including old suitcases and abandoned shoes. She recycled everything, effortlessly. And gradually she had only a small amount of stuff—mostly stuff her children gave her: nightgowns, perfume, a microwave—to recycle or to use.

Each time I visited her I marveled at the modesty of her desires. She appeared to have hardly any, beyond a thirst for a Pepsi-Cola or a hunger for a piece of fried chicken or fish. On every visit I noticed that more and more of what I remembered of her possessions seemed to be missing. One day I commented on this.

Taking a deep breath, sighing, and following both with a beaming big smile, which lit up her face, the room, and my heart, she said: Yes, it's all going. I don't need it anymore. If there's anything you want, take it when you leave; it might not be here when you come back.

The dishes my mother and father used daily had come from my house; I had sent them years before, when I moved from Mississippi to New York. Neither the plates nor the silver matched entirely, but it was all beautiful in her eyes. There were numerous paper items, used in the microwave, and stacks of plastic plates and cups, used by the scores of children from the neighborhood who continued throughout her life to come and go. But there was nothing there for me to want.

One day, however, looking for a jar into which to pour leftover iced tea, I found myself probing deep into the wilderness of the overstuffed, airless pantry. Into the land of the old-fashioned, the outmoded, the outdated. The humble and the obsolete. There was a smoothing iron, a churn. A butter press. And two large bowls.

One was cream and rose with a blue stripe. The other was a deep, vivid blue.

May I have this bowl, Mama, I asked, looking at her and at the blue bowl with delight.

You can have both of them, she said, barely acknowledging them, and continuing to put leftover food away.

I held the bowls on my lap for the rest of the evening, while she watched a TV program about cops and criminals that I found too horrifying to follow.

Before leaving the room I kissed her on the forehead and asked if I could get anything for her from the kitchen; then I went off to bed. The striped bowl I placed on a chair beside the door, so I could look at it from where I lay. The blue bowl I placed in the bed with me.

In giving me these gifts, my mother had done a number of astonishing things, in her typically offhand way. She had taught me a lesson about letting go of possessions—easily, without emphasis or regret—and she had given me a symbol of what she herself represented in my life.

For the blue bowl especially was a cauldron of memories. Of cold, harsh, wintry days, when my brothers and sister and I trudged home from school burdened down by the silence and frigidity of our long trek from the main road, down the hill to our shabby-looking house. More rundown than any of our classmates' houses. In winter my mother's riotous flowers would be absent, and the shack stood revealed for what it was. A gray, decaying, too small barrack meant to house the itinerant tenant workers on a prosperous white man's farm.

Slogging through sleet and wind to the sagging front door, thankful that our house was too far from the road to be seen clearly from the school bus, I always felt a wave of embarrassment and misery. But then I would open the door. And there inside would be my mother's winter flowers: a glowing fire in the fireplace, colorful handmade quilts on all our beds, paintings and drawings of flowers and fruits and, yes, of Jesus, given to her by who knows whom—and, most of all, there in the center of the rough-hewn table, which in the tiny kitchen almost touched the rusty wood-burning stove, stood the big blue bowl, full of whatever was the most tasty thing on earth.

There was my mother herself. Glowing. Her teeth sparkling. Her eyes twinkling. As if she lived in a castle and her favorite princes and princesses had just dropped by to visit.

The blue bowl stood there, seemingly full forever, no matter how deeply or rapaciously we dipped, as if it had no bottom. And she dipped up soup. Dipped up lima beans. Dipped up stew. Forked out potatoes. Spooned out rice and peas and corn. And in the light and warmth that was *Her*, we dined.

Thank you, Mama

Minnie Tallulah Grant Walker and Willie Lee Walker

PHOTO BY ITINERANT PHOTOGRAPHER
IN THE THIRTIES. EATONTON, GEORGIA

For your bravery,
commitment
and love,
your daughter
thanks you.

Your belief in the love
of the world,
against all odds
and evidence,
is the fire
that lights
my path.

<u>*Vencerémos!*</u>[*]

[*] *We shall overcome.*

ABOUT THE AUTHOR

ALICE WALKER was born in Eatonton, Georgia, and now lives in Northern California. Her novel *The Color Purple* won an American Book Award and the Pulitzer Prize.